I0113361

Alessandro Michele

FASHION AUTEURS

Series Editors
Adam Geczy and Vicki Karaminas

Fashion Auteurs is a groundbreaking book series devoted to designers who have left an indelible mark on fashion history. Critical, clear and concise, each title, comprising around 30K words, is written by authorities in the field, situating each designer within their time and against their peers, with a focus on the contributions that have made them memorable. Using the term 'auteur' to designate film directors with a distinctive and influential style, this is the first series to treat fashion designers and related fashion creators (e.g. photographers) as on par with artists who have decisively shaped imagery, taste, and what is seen to be current and desirable. These books will be of interest not only to fashionistas and ardent devotees of fashion magazines but also to students and teachers of art and design, artists and designers themselves, not to mention anyone seeking a deeper acquaintance with fashion and design culture.

Forthcoming Titles in the Series
Georgina Ripley, *Ray Petri*
Benjamin Wild, *Thom Browne*
Yuniya Kawamura, *Sebastian Masuda*

Ovidiu Hrubaru / Alamy Stock Photo

Alessandro Michele

Judith Beyer

ANTHEM PRESS

Anthem Press
An imprint of Wimbledon Publishing Company
www.anthempress.com

This edition first published in UK and USA 2026
by ANTHEM PRESS
75–76 Blackfriars Road, London SE1 8HA, UK
or PO Box 9779, London SW19 7ZG, UK
and
244 Madison Ave #116, New York, NY 10016, USA

© 2026 Judith Beyer

The author asserts the moral right to be identified as the author of this work.

All rights reserved. Without limiting the rights under copyright reserved above,
no part of this publication may be reproduced, stored or introduced into
a retrieval system, or transmitted, in any form or by any means
(electronic, mechanical, photocopying, recording or otherwise),
without the prior written permission of both the copyright
owner and the above publisher of this book.

British Library Cataloguing-in-Publication Data
A catalogue record for this book is available from the British Library.

Library of Congress Cataloging-in-Publication Data: 2025941262
A catalog record for this book has been requested.

ISBN-13: 978-1-83999-604-7 (Hbk) / 978-1-83999-605-4 (Pbk)
ISBN-10: 1-83999-604-8 (Hbk) / 1-83999-605-6 (Pbk)

This title is also available as an eBook.

CONTENTS

LIST OF FIGURES

ACKNOWLEDGEMENTS

I would like to thank the *Fashion Auteurs* series editors, Adam Geczy and Vicki Karaminas, for their insightful guidance and steadfast support throughout the development of this book. Special thanks also to the editorial and production teams and to all those – colleagues, peers, and friends – who offered their time, expertise, and encouragement along the way.

INTRODUCTION

Since his appointment as creative director of Gucci in 2015, Alessandro Michele has fostered an intellectual and influential design approach, a geek-chic aesthetic reminiscent of the fashion eccentric who wears flea market finds with high-end designer and heirloom pieces: imperfect, romantic and maximalist. While his creative output and direction of Gucci resulted in the financial and cultural success for the brand, his debut and tenure at Gucci were not without its critique. When he first showed his creations in front of the Milan audience in February 2015, all signs indicated that this would remain a one-off collection, partly because the events leading up to his appointment were anything but promising. Only ten days prior to the menswear show for Fall/Winter 2015/2016, Gucci's then creative director Frida Giannini left the company without completing her collection. Her sudden departure came just a few weeks after her partner, Gucci's CEO Patrizio di Marco, involuntary left the brand at the end of 2014. It was François-Henri Pinault, chairman of Gucci's parent company Kering, who replaced di Marco with Marco Bizzarri, former CEO at Stella McCartney and Bottega Veneta, in the hopes of putting an end to the faltering sales at Gucci. The brand had become stale and stagnated for too long, unable to continue the period of growth and cultural relevancy that Tom Ford and CEO Domenico de Sole had fostered between 1994 and 2004.

The newly appointed CEO Marco Bizzarri was tasked with finding a new creative lead fast and his preliminary choice fell on the relatively unknown Michele who had worked as Gucci's leather goods designer and later associate to Giannini for the last twelve years. At that time, however, Michele's first solo gig as creative director seemed a temporary solution. Several well-known designers were still rumoured to be in the race as Giannini's successor, from Givenchy's Riccardo Tisci and Peter Dundas from rival luxury group Louis Vuitton Moët Hennessy (LVMH) to Tom Ford himself, who had already regenerated the brand in the 1990s, although his return was always doubtful.

Consequently, the reviews for Michele's rapidly assembled collection were rather reserved, while enthralled by the collection's apparent nonconformist romanticism, *Vogue's* fashion writer Tim Blanks was also puzzled by its ambiguity. Smugly remarking that 'the very deliberate sissiness' of Michele's first collection was 'a glaringly obvious way to distance' the collection from Gucci's preceding ones, while also questioning its potential to become a 'launchpad for the label's next incarnation'.[1] Michele's first collection was a motley mix of nerdy glasses and bobble hats, pussy bow blouses and lace tops, grandma's Persian lamb coat and fur-lined home slippers and shrunken jackets with too-short sleeves that left many wondering if its lack of a clearly identifiable design language could revive the brand. However, it was to become a precursor for Michele's romantic eclecticism, postmodern sensibility and 'visceral storytelling through fashion' as the Fall/Winter 2015/2016 show notes claimed; a first look at his penchant to plunder and rework historic references, cultural motifs, and gender signifiers. 'I do not do fashion', Michele said, 'I design a way to live'.[2]

It was his 'way to live' that was a crucial factor in Bizzarri's ensuing choice to name Michele as Gucci's new creative director just a few days after his inaugural collection. In a surprising decision, he granted Michele total control not only for Gucci's menswear and womenswear collections, but accessories, eyewear, jewellery and children's wear, the beauty and fragrance departments, advertising, digital and social media platforms as well as store design – virtually giving him more responsibility and power over a brand than any other creative director had at the time. While Bizzarri's choice was surprising for the fashion world, it was no less surprising for Michele himself who had already made plans to leave the company at the time. During a meeting at Michele's apartment in Rome in December 2014, where they initially planned to discuss ways to improve working processes, Michele and Bizzarri began to discuss the brand's image and visions for the future. As Michele emphasized, it was his style of furnishings and interior that tipped the scale for Bizzarri, who was baffled by his collection of antique furniture, artworks and figurines that line the walls of the space and questioned whether it was Michele's living room or some kind of museum. 'I orchestrate my life', Michele said, 'to make it a work of art'[3] – a sentiment he would later apply to Gucci as well, completely reinventing the brand's visual codes and creating an all-encompassing aesthetic world.

Having made the decision to leave the company, Michele agreed to re-design Giannini's last collection, Gucci's Fall/Winter 2015/2016 menswear, in only a few days. Seemingly overnight Michele changed the fashion house's visual codes completely. Gone were the days of Giannini's carefully cultivated glamour and Ford's overt sexuality and hedonism. Instead, a ragtag crew of misfit geeks and androgynous men flocked Michele's runway, dressed in idiosyncratic vintage looks and mismatched accessories. While Giannini's focus was on Gucci's heritage, redesigning archival pieces for a modern, cool and sophisticated clientele, Michele seemed to have thrown out the rules of good taste, creating patchwork vintage looks that boldly played with the concepts of luxury fashion, heritage, and intellectualism.

With the accompanying text for the Fall/Winter 2015/2016 womenswear collection Michele overhauled the concept of the ritualized fashion show and introduced the collection with a short philosophical essay, quoting and pondering over words by Giorgio Agamben and Roland Barthes. A decision that would become a habit: The texts, which he wrote together with his partner Giovanni Attili, a professor for urban planning, would accompany every collection and combine the discourse of fashion and art with the philosophy of Michel Foucault, Hannah Arendt or Donna J. Haraway. By introducing his designs with these philosophical underpinnings, he not only accepted and promoted the need of philosophy to understand and talk about fashion, but elevated fashion itself to a form of philosophy. Discovering these philosophical concepts that spoke to and enhanced his own understanding of clothes was like 'discovering a new language, an unexplored territory, a space of consciousness', as he would later write in *The Life of Forms: Theory of the Re-enchantment* (original title: *La vita della forma: Filosofia del reincanto*, 2024). The book, which he wrote together with Italian philosopher Emanuele Coccia after he had left Gucci, offers a reflection on the core principles and thoughts that have shaped Michele's practice. 'Just as fashion is nothing other than the totality of the means and procedures by which a life attempts to reinvent its form', Michele writes, 'philosophy is nothing other than the totality of desires and knowledge that enable us to live more intensely'.[4]

Fashion critics were hesitant to embrace Michele's new Gucci by the time of his first womenswear show as the official new creative director. As Nicole Phelps writes in *Vogue*, the collection overall expressed youthful naïveté, though 'as playful and irreverent as it was, it lacked a bit for sophistication'.

Nonetheless, it became clear 'that he wrapped a lot of the audience in his poetic embrace'.[5] That he finally won the favour of the customers and fashion writers would ring true only a few months later, when Gucci's sales started to rise. While its annual revenue was 3.5 billion Euros by the end of 2014 when Michele took over from Giannini, its sales increased continuously with revenues in the fourth quarter up by 5 per cent compared to the previous year.[6] By the end of 2021, nearing the end of Michele's tenure at Gucci, the brand had almost tripled its revenue during his time as creative director, with sales nearly reaching 9.8 billion Euros.[7] Although Michele's overhaul of Gucci seemed to be a risky step at first, his time at the fashion house turned out to be a success story, also in part due to his ability to capture the cultural zeitgeist.

From Normcore to Gender Fluidity

While Michele's mix-and-match approach was not an entirely new concept, his misfit aesthetic came at a time when the reactionary years of austerity in response to the global economic crisis of 2008 wore off. The early years of the 2010s were characterized by the mainstreaming of minimalism and normcore aesthetics. Normcore, coined by the New York-based trend forecasting agency K-Hole in 2013 primarily described an attitude that, rather than emphasizing individuality and distinction, focuses on adaptability, belonging and normality. Freedom, within a normcore mindset, meant not having to be anything or anyone special. This attitude translated into a unisex fashion consisting of minimalist everyday pieces like t-shirts, hoodies, denim jeans or chinos. With the increasing rise of social media, fashion bloggers and influencers, the focus on normality and fitting in started to shift. Michele's Gucci unabashedly celebrated embellishment, maximalist and eclectic styling and met the spirit of the time that longed for individuality rather than conformity. Although the widespread success of Michele's design raised the question of true individuality, his collections were not designed as cohesive outfits to be sold as one, but as a continuum of single garments that could be mixed and matched to suit the wearer's taste and personality.

It was not only the yearning for individual expression that resonated with the fashion crowd, but Michele's total disregard of the gender binary, his gender-fluid or rather antigender fashion design.[8] His new vision of Gucci is firmly situated within the context of a growing transgender movement and visibility. Ongoing activism by trans*, non-binary and gender non-confirming people resulted in increasing visibility on and off the runway, ensuring that the term transgender had 'entered mainstream consciousness' in 2015.[9] Consequently, Michele's gender-fluid fashion design – a design that transcends, combines and decontextualizes gender signifiers – 'jump-started a revolution', a seismic shift that 'ushered gender fluidity into fashion' and, one might argue, society at large.[10]

While the topic of transgender and in more acute ways, trans* people and their bodies, have become the latest battlefield for right-wing movements, fascist formations and emerging authoritarian regimes in recent years,[11] the beginning of the 2010s saw a more widespread representation of gender diversity through an increasing number of transgender and gender non-conforming models on runways and in fashion advertising campaigns. For instance, Ricardo Tisci's 2010 campaign for Givenchy featuring transgender model Lea T, or Andreja Pejic, whose career did not falter after her transition. Nonetheless, the growing presence of transgender and gender non-conforming models also created a challenge to the hyper-expressions of gender and sexuality that were at the foreground in the early 2000s. While androgyny and a minimalistic unisex aesthetic were central to mainstream fashion at the turn of the millennium, the following years marked a shift towards a heightened focus on hyper-femininity and hyper-masculinity, epitomized by phenomena like the 'spornosexual' or the exaggerated physiques of Marvel's superhero actors and James Bond.[12]

In the course of the 2010s, fuelled and formed by social media, several social rights movements took shape, such as the Black Lives Matter protests, the #MeToo campaign that addresses sexual abuse and harassment and climate protest groups Fridays for Future and Extinction Rebellion. The transgender rights movement resulted in a growing number of films, television series and fashion campaigns featuring diverse and inclusive models and actors. It was shortly after the height of the transgender rights movement – that *Time* magazine coined 'The Transgender Tipping Point' on its May 2014 cover featuring a full-body portrait of African American transgender actress Laverne Cox. This occurred at the time when Michele showed his first collection.

Breaking with his predecessor's sleek sophistication, Michele's first collection challenged conventional notions of gender and beauty. The menswear collection featured vintage-inspired tailoring, chiffon blouses with pussycat bows, fitted knitwear, and sheer lace tops. Most strikingly, the menswear and womenswear collection blurred gender lines, with traditionally feminine garments worn by models 'irrespective of gender', including chiffon dresses, pleated skirts, and ruffled tops.[13] This fluid approach to aesthetics and gender marked the beginning of Michele's distinctive vision for Gucci's gender-fluid fashion. As fashion journalist Yari Fiocca observed, 'Michele keeps through the thrills of bending sexes, creating a more flamboyant halo with a 70s style throwback. His off-gender brave new world confuses, winks. Male or female is just a hangover of the past'.[14]

Michele's off-gender brave new world struck a chord with fashion critics and costumers alike and cemented Gucci as 'a lynchpin brand in the gender-free movement'.[15] Tim Blanks, who was cautious to call Michele's first show a success for Gucci, adopted a different tone in his review of the Spring/Summer 2016 menswear collection, welcoming instead 'the New Punk': 'Alessandro Michele has brought a radically different culture to Gucci [...]. If it isn't exactly new, the magpie sensibility of Michele's Gucci – scouring time, place, and gender for scraps [...] That, in itself, is punk'.[16]

Commenting on his inclination for breaking gender norms, Michele attributed his fluid design approach to his own sense of beauty, postulating that life and beauty are always ambiguous 'in the truest sense of the word. For this means being more than one thing at the same time, or rather, having a form that can never be reduced to a single meaning'.[17] For Michele it is not just the multifaceted character of beauty that inspired his fluid fashion design, but rather beauty itself that 'multiplies lives. Beauty endows the forms of the world with unexpected and imponderable possibilities, blurs the geometries of identities, shortens the distances between them, and defines a common space, a communal world'.[18] In many ways, this is what defines Michele's work as a fashion auteur: the sheer endless possibilities of fashion and its forms, the breaking apart of it and reassembling in always new yet old ways. As Michele writes in *The Life of Forms*:

> All my collections attempt to evoke this magic. In each of them, I have pursued an ideal of beauty and ambiguity that revives in bodies forgotten identities: a garment must allow each face to express more than one life. To achieve this, from the very beginning, I mixed physiognomies, hybridizing everything I encountered: for me, it was a way to integrate diversity into each individual form. It wasn't something artificial to achieve a particular effect; rather, I instinctively sought to breathe multiple lives back into the reality around me.[19]

It was this hybridity, the bold accessories, flowing dresses, floral prints, and chiffon bows worn across genders that had a lasting impact on Gucci and the fashion world. Michele's work challenged and challenges traditional notions of gender (as well as time and place) and introduced a new chapter in fashion design, where gender becomes less of a boundary and more of a fluid, creative interplay.[20] Rather than downplaying gender signifiers, Michele's gender-fluid fashion adorns, embellishes and flaunts gender, creating a story of beauty as ambiguous as it is fluid.

From Rome to London and Milan

Born in Rome in 1972, Michele's family and life in the so-called eternal city was an early influence on his poetic sensibility and visceral storytelling. His father, while a technician at Italian airline Alitalia by profession, was a devotee of the arts who saw his true vocation in sculpture, music and poetry. 'He played more than ten instruments and wrote poems and stories' said Michele.[21] His mother was an executive assistant at a film production company in Rome and loved classic cinema and the Golden Age of Hollywood, including actresses like Lauren Becall and Bette Davis. While it was his mother who instilled in him a love for the beauty of appearance, it was his mother's twin, his 'super-stylish' Aunt Giuliana who fostered his love for clothes. A film editor in the 1970s, she was 'totally obsessed with fashion' recounts Michele. 'She'd spend all her money on Chanel furs, dresses and platform shoes. I was in love with her, and I guess she introduced me to the idea that you could transform yourself through clothes'.[22]

With the intention of becoming a costume designer, Michele went on to study costume design at Rome's Academy of Costume and Fashion. In 1994, aged 22, he eventually shifted towards fashion and started working at the Italian knitwear company Les Copains in Bologna. Three years later, he went back to Rome to work in the accessories department at Fendi, then under the creative direction of Karl Lagerfeld and Silvia Venturini Fendi, who in 1997 designed the infamous Fendi Baguette bag which would later become an important source of inspiration for Michele. As he writes,

> This bag was wrapped in stories, places, countries, houses, faces, and people from elsewhere. This was an important training for me, because it made me realize that fashion can present and embody any narrative, that it can communicate the story of any person and anything, with free choice of form and process.[23]

In 2002, Gucci's creative director at the time, Tom Ford, invited Michele to work at Gucci's accessories department in London, alongside Frida Giannini, who worked as head of design for handbags and accessories. In a subtle homage to Ford, Michele would later choose Abel Korzeniowski's theme music from *A Single Man* (2009), Ford's directorial debut, as the soundtrack for his first collection for Gucci. In 2006, after Giannini took over womenswear and menswear, he was promoted to senior designer of Gucci's leather goods before becoming associate director to Giannini in 2011. In 2014, before taking the reins at Gucci, Michele became the creative director for Richard Ginori, a Florentine porcelain brand founded in 1735 that was acquired by Gucci the previous year.

It seems only fitting that his love for porcelain and his collector's passion would lead Michele to head a porcelain brand. However, it did not end there: In 2017, Gucci launched its first home décor line, Gucci Décor. Consisting of a variety of pieces, from scented candles in porcelain jars, trays, cushions, and mugs to lacquered chairs with embroidered upholstery, double-sided folding screens and tapestry. The pieces, designed by Michele, featured the by then well-known Gucci motifs, patterns and codes, including drawings of cats and tigers, floral patterns, and stylized sketches of eyes. Some of the porcelain pieces, including the vases, were produced by Richard Ginori, while the *capitonné* porter's chair was inspired by the high-backed chairs used in England and sixteenth-century France. The Gucci Décor line offered a way to dress your own home in Michele's pop-meets-renaissance aesthetic.

Similarly extensive and all-encompassing was the refurbishment of the Gucci Museum in Florence, re-opened in January 2018 as the Gucci Garden. The concept store/museum is housed in the Palazzo della Mercanzia in Florence's Piazza Signoria that dates to 1337. Besides a boutique selling exclusive pieces designed for the Gucci Garden and the museum, there is a small cinema that screens art-house movies. Then there is Gucci Osteria, the first restaurant by the brand and managed by three-star executive chef Massimo Bottura. Spanning over two floors and six themed rooms, the so-called Gucci Garden Galleria recounts the history of the fashion house with clothes, accessories and archival pieces as well as displays of the vision and codes of Michele's Gucci. The Gucci Eye, a neon-sign of a sketched eye installed on the façade of the Palazzo, is not only the symbol for the Gucci Garden, but emblematic of Michele's cross-cultural and cross-temporal design approach.

Michele's unconventional design approach to the heritage brand was recognized at the end of 2015 when the British Fashion Council awarded him the 2015 International Designer Award. One year later, he won the International Award 'for his creative contribution to the international fashion stage' from the Council of Fashion Designers of America (CFDA), and the British Gentlemen's Quarterly (GQ) Designer of the Year Award. After seven successful years at the helm of Gucci, the brand announced Michele's departure in November 2022. The news came after a *Women's Wear Daily* article was published quoting sources saying that Michele did not meet the request of parent company Kering, whose CEO François-Henri Pinault was seeking a change in pace for the brand.[24] In a statement released by the company, Michele offered his thanks to the team at Gucci, commenting that 'there are times when paths part ways because of the different perspectives each one of us may have'.[25]

Two years later, in March 2024, Valentino appointed Michele as the new creative director, shortly after Pierpaolo Piccolio's exit at the brand a week prior. Piccolio had been at Valentino for more than two decades, joining in 1999 alongside Maria Grazia Chiuri. In 2008, the two became co-creative directors before Piccolio took on the role of sole creative director in 2016, when Chiuri moved to Dior. The fashion house, founded by Valentino Garavani in 1960, offered Michele a vast archive to plunder and reassemble. However, with the Maison Valentino, Michele also began his foray into Haute Couture, showing his first couture collection in January 2025. The way the designer adapted his maximalist design philosophy to the context of the heritage fashion house of Valentino will be examined in greater depth in Chapter 4 of this book.

Structuring Alessandro Michele's body of work presents a challenge, as its elements are deeply interconnected – each aspect influencing and evolving in a complex, often temporally dislocated and eclectic manner. Rather than following a strictly chronological or thematic order, I have chosen to organize this book around three overarching concepts. The first chapter, *Fluid Futures*, explores Michele's approach to gender and identity, particularly his embrace of fluidity – not only in terms of gender expression but also in his treatment of time and cultural signifiers. Although positioned at the beginning, the core ideas introduced in this chapter permeate his entire oeuvre, forming a conceptual foundation for the chapters that follow. The second chapter, *Bizarre Beauty*, investigates Michele's reimagining of beauty – its distortions, transformations, and the embrace of a surreal, often uncanny aesthetic. While the discussion centres on a selection of specific collections, the principle of 'bizarre beauty' is a recurring motif that defines much of his creative output. The third chapter, *Hacking Heritage*, addresses Michele's ongoing dialogue with other creatives, focusing on his collaborations and his complex engagement with brand heritage. This includes his integration of archival references and historical signifiers, in his tenure at Gucci and, as is the focus of Chapter 4, in his more recent work at Valentino. Through this lens, Michele's work emerges as a layered conversation between past and present, between structure and fluidity, self and other.

Notes

1 Tim Blanks, 'Gucci Fall 2015 Menswear', *Vogue*, 19 January 2015, https://www.vogue.com/fashion-shows/fall-2015-menswear/gucci.

2 Brenda Polan and Roger Tredre, *The Great Fashion Designers: From Chanel to McQueen, the Names that Made Fashion History*, 2nd ed. (London: Bloomsbury Visual Arts, 2020), 363.

3 Michael Ebert and Sven Michaelsen, 'Alessandro Michele: Das Interview', *Fashion Icons*, Die Gucci Story – Wie Alessandro Michele die Modewelt verändert, no. 01 (2019): 25.

4 Emanuele Coccia and Alessandro Michele, *Das Leben der Formen: Eine Philosophie der Wiederverzauberung*, trans. Thomas Stauder (München: Hanser, 2025), 32–33, my translation.

5 Nicole Phelps, 'Gucci Fall 2015 Ready-to-Wear', *Vogue*, 25 February 2015, https://www.vogue.com/fashion-shows/fall-2015-ready-to-wear/gucci.

6 Kering, '2015 Results', news release, 19 February 2016, https://www.
   kering.com/en/news/2015-results-solid-full-year-performances/.

7 Kering, *2021 Financial Document*, Kering (Kering, 17 February 2022),
   16. https://www.kering.com/api/download-file/?path=Kering_2021_
   Financial_Document_ENG_4fa3b7a30c.pdf.

8 Judith Beyer, *Antigender Fashion: The Possibilities of Gender-Fluid and Non-
   Binary Fashion Design* (London: Bloomsbury Visual Arts, 2025).

9 Brendon Griggs, 'America's Transgender Moment', *CNN*, 1 June 2015,
   https://edition.cnn.com/2015/04/23/living/transgender-moment-
   jenner-feat/index.html.

10 Lynn Hirschberg, 'Alessandro Michele Reflects on Making a Gucci
   Collection in One Week," *W Magazine*, 2 February 2020, https://
   www.wmagazine.com/story/gucci-alessandro-michele-interview.

11 Judith Butler, *Who's Afraid of Gender?* (Great Britain: Allen Lane /
   Penguin Books, 2024).

12 Sarah Goldsmith, 'Marble Marvels and Classical Ideals', in *Fashioning
   Masculinities: The Art of Menswear*, ed. Rosalind McKever, Claire
   Wilcox, and Marta Franceschini (London: V&A Publishing, 2022);
   Pamela Church Gibson, 'The Rough and the Smooth Revisited:
   Masculintiy, Fashion, and James Bond for a New Millennium', in
   Fashionable Masculinities. Queer, Pimp Daddies and Lumbersexuals, ed.
   Vicki Karaminas, Adam Geczy, and Pamela Church Gibson (New
   Brunswick, New Jersey: Rutgers University Press, 2022).

13 Vicki Karaminas and Justine Taylor, 'Harry Styles: Fashion's
   Gender Changeling', in *Fashionable Masculinities. Queer, Pimp Daddies
   and Lumbersexuals*, ed. Vicki Karaminas, Adam Geczy, and Pamela
   Church Gibson (New Brunswick, New Jersey: Rutgers University
   Press, 2022), 16.

14 Patrick Mauriès, *Androgyne: Fashion + Gender* (London: Thames &
   Hudson, 2017), 154.

15 Zak Maoui, 'Gender Fluid Fashion is the Future. Here's How
   Menswear is Changing', *GQ*, 27 November 2018, https://www.
   gq-magazine.co.uk/article/gender-fluid-clothing.

16 Tim Blanks, 'Gucci Spring 2016 Menswear', *Vogue*, 22 June 2015, https://www.vogue.com/fashion-shows/spring-2016-menswear/gucci.

17 Coccia and Michele, *Das Leben der Formen: Eine Philosophie der Wiederverzauberung*, 54.

18 Ibid., 55.

19 Ibid., 60.

20 Beyer, *Antigender Fashion: The Possibilities of Gender-Fluid and Non-Binary Fashion Design*, 123.

21 Ebert and Michaelsen, 'Alessandro Michele: Das Interview', 22.

22 Jonathan Wingfield, 'The Happy Couple: Marco Bizzarri & Alessandro Michele', *System Magazine*, 2016, https://system-magazine.com/issues/issue-7/alessandro-michele-marco-bizzarri.

23 Coccia and Michele, *Das Leben der Formen: Eine Philosophie der Wiederverzauberung*, 111.

24 Luisa Zargani, 'Alessandro Michele Is Exiting Gucci, Sources Say', *Women's Wear Daily*, 22 November 2022, https://wwd.com/fashion-news/designer-luxury/sources-say-alessandro-michele-exiting-gucci-1235427822/.

25 Kering. 'Alessandro Michele stepping down as Gucci's Creative Director'. *Kering*, 2022, accessed 27 January 2025, https://www.kering.com/en/news/alessandro-michele-stepping-down-as-gucci-s-creative-director/.

Chapter 1

FLUID FUTURE

In January 2019, Gucci premiered at the Sundance Film Festival with the short film *The Future is Fluid*. In partnership with Chime for Change, a global campaign founded in 2013 by Gucci in collaboration with Beyoncé Knowles Carter and Selma Hayek Pinault, the campaign intended to raise awareness and funds for women and girls and gender equality. The short film deals with the concept of gender fluidity through the experience of 13 teenagers and young adults. Directed by Jade Jackman and Irregular Labs, the film explores what gender means to Gen-Z around the world, featuring individuals from Brazil, Canada, India, Italy, the United Arab Emirates, the United Kingdom, Singapore and South Africa. In the film, the youth speak about the challenges and opportunities of gender and fluidity, how it impacts, creates and inspires their everyday lives. In the press release, Gucci explains that the film aims to tell 'the story of a generation who demand to live in a world that is free', adding that the voices in the film are 'redefining and representing the world through a prism of fluidity'.[1]

To redefine and represent, 'the world through a prism of fluidity' could also be the motto of Alessandro Michele's fashion design, not just fluidity in terms of gender, but fluidity of time, places and all kinds of cultural references. While Michele's fluid approach to gender might have caught a lot of attention at first, it is his sense of fluidity, freedom and the juxtaposition of disparate signs that defines his eclectic and romantic aesthetic as a fashion auteur. In an interview, Michele explained his design philosophy at the beginning of his tenure as Gucci's creative director:

> It was more a case of expressing romanticism [...] or simply the idea of freedom. [...] My way of working is to put things together and create a kind of chemical reaction. I feel that by taking fragments that are apparently dead and putting them together in new ways, you create something modern and beautiful.[2]

It is, perhaps, this fragmentation of signs and signifiers that best describes Michele's design approach – and that also speaks to the difficulties in pinpointing his aesthetic. Just as his designs stem from several sources and inspirations, his collections and designs evade a clear and singular definition. From his first catwalk show, the Fall/Winter 2015/2016 menswear collection entitled 'Urban Romanticism', Michele showed his models in looks that could have been plucked from your grandparents' wardrobes, freely mixing masculine and feminine signs like pussy bow blouses, sheer fabrics and lace worn by men and women. He continued this fluid approach in the Fall/Winter 2015/2016 womenswear collection, showing pink pussy bow blouses and floral shrunken suits.

Gucci Fall/Winter 2015/2016

Michele's first two collections were the introduction to his romantic, intellectual, vintage-inspired fashion design that, in course of his career, would become even more pronounced and colourful. However, the beginning was still presented in muted colours, consisting mostly of earthy green and brown shades with occasional bright pinks, reds and blues. The colour scheme contributed to the overall impression that the pieces were found in a vintage shop and worn together with a motley assortment of accessories like knitted bobble hats, berets and horn-rimmed glasses. With their quirky and eccentric styling (mismatched pieces, shrunken sleeves and voluminous coats), Michele's models seemed to have escaped Wes Anderson's world in *The Royal Tenenbaums* (2001).

In other words, Michele's models appear as fleshed-out characters, as part of a larger story realised through fashion. As the designer explains, his approach to creating a collection is like writing a film script, it is not just based on imagining singular garments, but the people and stories that are embodied within them:

> When I work, I almost never think about just one piece of clothing: I'm immediately immersed in a narrative involving numerous characters. It's as if I were writing the script for a film: little by little, faces and possible lives, atmospheres, and relationships between the characters emerge.[3]

For his debut collection, the lives he imagined took place in a specific urban landscape, in cities like New York, Paris or London. Michele's characters would stroll through the city streets, encounter each other briefly at stop lights, on the subway or spend their time drinking and laughing at a bar. They would wear garments found in thrift shops and pieces they inherited from their grandmothers. They would put on bobble hats if it were cold and worn-in suit pants if they went out.

What was most striking was that all the models wore the same chiffon blouses, fur coats and sheer lace tops regardless of their gender. With his first two collections, Michele introduced a new aesthetic to Gucci that stood in stark contrast to his predecessor Tom Ford's sexy, hedonistic and glamorous vision of the brand and established Gucci as one of the most visible and talked about fashion houses incorporating gender fluidity. Or, as Lynn Hirschberg writes, Michele 'jump-started a revolution' and 'ushered gender fluidity into fashion'.[4]

A key item in this revolution was the bright red pussy bow blouse that adorned the very first look of Michele's debut collection. Envisioning a 'young man with long hair and lilies of the valley on his head, wearing a red shirt with a *lavallière* and black trousers',[5] Michele introduced a new approach to challenging gendered fashion, one that exists in-between and against the binary of masculinity/femininity, one that celebrates and exaggerates the ambiguity of gender fluidity. While other gender-bending fashions strive to unify or neutralize masculine and feminine styles by blending sartorial signs into a supposedly neutral unisex or androgynous style, it often relies on and overemphasizes the presumed neutrality of masculine clothing styles and characteristics.[6] Michele's new vision of gender-fluid fashion, in contrast, plays with and celebrates the ambiguity of garments and styles endowed with multiple meanings and gendered signifiers. The so-called *lavallière* is a prime example of Michele's gender-fluid and antigender fashion.

The *lavallière* is a wide, soft bow tied around the neck with long, loose ends that became popular in the second half of the nineteenth century. In the 1880s, it became a popular accessory amongst artists and bohemians after French painter Henri de Toulouse-Lautrec, famous for depicting local artists, singers and showgirls, drew a dancer with such a bow.[7] In the course of the twentieth century, the *lavallière* – also called pussycat bow or pussy bow as it has sometimes been likened to the bow placed around the necks of pussy cats – became associated with power dressing and the feminine subversion of male spaces. As Fleur Britten writes, 'The 1960s pussybow gave women working in a man's world a soft-power version of a suit and tie. [...] It was an iron fist in a velvet glove'.[8] Following Coco Chanel's use of silk pussy bows to soften the structured look of fabrics like tweed, Yves Saint Laurent's infamous tuxedo for women *Le Smoking* designed in 1966 – even more so Helmut Newton's fashion shoot for the French *Vogue* in 1975 that featured an androgynous model in a YSL tuxedo with a soft pussy bow, standing hazily lit in a Parisian alleyway – helped mythicize the pussy bow blouse as a radically subversive and feminist garment. During her tenure as prime minister of the United Kingdom, the pussycat bow was a staple in Margaret Thatcher's wardrobe, increasing its association with women's power dressing.[9] The association of the *lavallière* with challenging traditional (feminine) dress codes and appropriating masculine attire is also connected to its namesake, duchess Louise de La Vallière, mistress of Louis XIV. Since the middle of the seventeenth century, so-called *cravates* were a widespread style at the French court. They were valuable scarves or neckties made from Venetian or Flemish lace and are considered to be the precursor of today's tie. The duchess took a liking to this men's fashion and began to wear a scarf tied in a bow around her own neck.

Michele's decision to dress a young man in a red pussy bow blouse is an inversion, a radical appropriation and recontextualization of the gendered signifier of the *lavallière* – an accessory that is neither just masculine nor feminine but that carries connotations of both. As Emanuele Coccia writes, 'This is more than just a stylistic innovation; it is a true anthropological revolution. It is not only the garment that is ambiguous; gender itself becomes a space of ambiguity'.[10] It is this fluid ambiguity that is at the heart of Michele's debut collection and that would fundamentally shape his designs:

> I believe that this fashion show has shaped my approach: it is as if, vacillating between different identities and between past and present, I had found a way to reconcile fashion with experience, with the world shared by women and men, with the life of the young man with the flowers on his head, whom each of us can see next to the traffic light in any city.[11]

The examination and re-examination of gender through dress and fashion have a long history. For instance, the boyish look of the flapper and the so-called *garçonne* in the 1920s marked a fashionable ideal in contrast to traditional feminine styles, incorporating masculine elements like tailored suits, bow ties and short hair. In the 1960s and 1970s, the exaggerated femininity of the 1950s gave way to a new, youthful and androgynous version of femininity, embodied for instance by British model Lesly Hornby (also known as Twiggy). Feminist, anti-war and other social movements at the time also shaped a convergence in men's and women's fashion, leading to expressive, psychedelic unisex aesthetics that questioned gender norms.[12]

By the 1990s and the turn of the millennium, fashion once again reflected shifting cultural and gender norms. Unisex styles re-emerged as minimalist workwear looks, as seen in Calvin Klein's CK One campaign, while designers like Hedi Slimane and Raf Simons reimagined menswear through sleek, androgynous silhouettes. It was in the 2010s, however, that genderless fashion became more prominent, coinciding with broader recognition of non-binary and queer identities.[13] With growing visibility of LGBTQIA+ narratives in media and the momentum of trans* rights movements, fashion began to move beyond binary definitions, creating space for new forms of self-expression and identity.

In the mid-2010s, Michele introduced his fluid design approach and established Gucci as a gender-fluid fashion brand with his ragtag crew of misfits and outsiders that seem to share the same wardrobe. What is at the forefront for Michele, however, is not the pursuit of gender fluidity per se – for him, gendered fashion and the divide between masculine/feminine, menswear/womenswear had simply run its course. Consequently, in 2016, Gucci announced that it would show the womenswear and menswear shows together, disregarding the industry's standards of separate fashion weeks and calendars. At the core, Michele's gender-fluid fashion design is part of his overall fluid approach to time, places and gender. 'My aesthetic philosophy', said Michele, 'is an uninterrupted flow: There is no distinction between old and new things, but there are only beautiful things'.[14]

Michele's concept of time is nonlinear and fluid, always moving between the past, present and imagined future. In the show notes for the Fall//Winter 2015/2016 womenswear collection, he explained his penchant for a nonlinear understanding of time with a quote by Italian philosopher Giorgio Agamben:

Those who are truly contemporary, who truly belong to their time, are those who neither perfectly coincide with it nor adjust themselves to its demands. They are thus in this sense irrelevant [*inattuale*]. But [...] precisely through this disconnection and this anachronism, they are more capable than others to perceiving and grasping their own time. [...] Contemporariness is [...] *that relationship with time that adheres to it through a disjunction.*[15]

The quote is taken from Agamben's well-known 2008 short book *Che cos'è il contemporaneo?* (English title: *What is the Contemporary?*). Transcribed from Agamben's inaugural course at his 2007 seminar at the European Graduate School, he begins by posing the question "'Of whom and of what are we contemporaries?" And, first and foremost, "What does it mean to be contemporary?"'.[16] In his opening remarks, he describes contemporariness not as belonging to a specific period of time, 'but as a coexistence of different times within a single time; the presence of something that – while belonging to a different time – is still present or is not yet there'.[17]

In this way, Agamben draws on Walter Benjamin's concept of the *dialektisches Bild*, the dialectical image, which brings together multiple moments of time, collapsing the distance between the past and the now, where 'what has been comes together in a flash with the now to form a constellation'.[18] The idea of the constellation offers a way to disrupt the linearity of time and serves as a critique of modern notions of history. Like Benjamin, who describes fashion as the tiger's leap into the past, Agamben offers fashion as an example of contemporariness. Accordingly, 'the time of fashion [...] constitutively anticipates itself and consequently is also always too late. It always takes the form of an ungraspable threshold between a "not yet" and a "no more"'. In other words, fashion 'recall[s], re-evoke[s], and revitalize[s]',[19] it does not move forward in a linear fashion of newness. Rather, fashion and the act of wearing fashion, carry with them multiple temporalities – the historical references embedded in the garment, the moments of their creation and the moment of wearing it. By wearing clothes, one embodies various times, existing between and beyond the present and the past: a convergence of different temporalities where the space between oneself and the now is filled with echoes of other times.

These echoes come into effect in Michele's Gucci Fall/ Winter 2015/2016 ready-to-wear collection. The models walked down the runway in an eclectic and eccentric mix of heirloom pieces like colourful coats with fur cuffs and military details, chunky rimmed glasses and pompom hats. Flowy, shapeless floral print dresses were mixed with shrunken tailored suits, as if they inherited these ill-fitting clothes, demonstrating the convergence of different temporalities. Many pieces had intentional creases at different places, at the hem of trousers, along the side of a jacket or spread over a blue pleated dress, once more emphasizing that these pieces have, or could have, existed in another time.

The recourse of styles and garments of the past was for Michele an act of contemporariness to ignite and inflame the current moment of experience. By using garments and pieces of clothing that are associated with specific forms of femininity (pussy bow blouses), of age (retro silhouettes), and of class (fur coats), and transferring them onto other bodies and genders, Michele created a (gender-)fluid reality charged with different temporalities and gendered signifiers. 'In this way', Michele writes,

> that earlier world, strongly connoted in terms of gender and social class, was able to come back to life: presented in a different context, with a different voice, grafted onto much younger bodies, this past shone anew. This is the essence of fashion: a rediscovery, a poetic spell. Creating clothes means exploding the words used by others and charging them with new meaning.[20]

Gucci Spring/Summer 2016

For his second menswear collection, Gucci Spring/Summer 2016 menswear, Michele continued his fluid approach to temporalities, gender and cultural references. Entitled *détournement*, meaning rerouting or hijacking in French, the collection was a re-contextualizing and a semiotic sabotage of signs. Relocated to the abandoned Farini Railway station at the outskirts of Milan, the show was once again a departure from the previous image of sleek sophistication and the sexy hedonism of Ford's Gucci. Instead, Michele's collection showed a composition – a constellation of historical references, Punk anti-aesthetics, gender fluidity and colourful patterns.

The first outfit on the runway was a look echoing the past with a long trench coat in Gucci's double G pattern and suede detailing, paired with a long blue silk scarf with a flower pattern reminiscent of 1970s Biba scarves, dark green flared pants and big horn-rimmed tinted glasses. Flower prints ran through the collection, adorning flared, tailored trousers, suit jackets and blouses. One beige-coloured lace shirt was embroidered with symmetrical floral garland in burnt orange along the collarbone. So-called *lavallières* or pussy bow ties were styled with structured trench coats or tailored suits. There was a green silk robe with shrunken sleeves and fur cuffs, a knitted white jumper with a butterfly and anchor motif and pyjama-like sets in soft pink wallpaper print with a doily around the neck. A tailored suit featured the so-called Gucci Tian print, a botanical pattern with birds and plants inspired by eighteenth-century Chinese wallpaper prints[21] (Figure 1.1). Other looks featured bleached denim shorts and trench coats or buttoned blouses with scattered flowers and skirts (for all genders). One look in particular exemplified Michele's fluid design approach: a light blue leather biker jacket adorned with metallic studs

Figure 1.1. Runway look from the Gucci Spring/Summer 2016 collection. The model is wearing the so-called 'Tian' suit (Photo: taniavolobueva/Shutterstock.com).

and embroidered with tattoo-like birds and flowers, combined with a blue *lavallière* shirt and golden silk trousers with flower details reminiscent of eighteenth-century patterned breeches and *justaucorps* (Figure 1.2). In other words, Michele's Spring/Summer 2016 menswear collection hijacked historical and gender signifiers, a *détournement.*

Developed by the Letterist International in the 1950s, and later adopted by the Situationists, *détournement* is a technique defined as the diversion of 'preexisting aesthetic elements. The integration of present or past artistic productions into a superior construction of a milieu'.[22] In other words, *détournement* is the

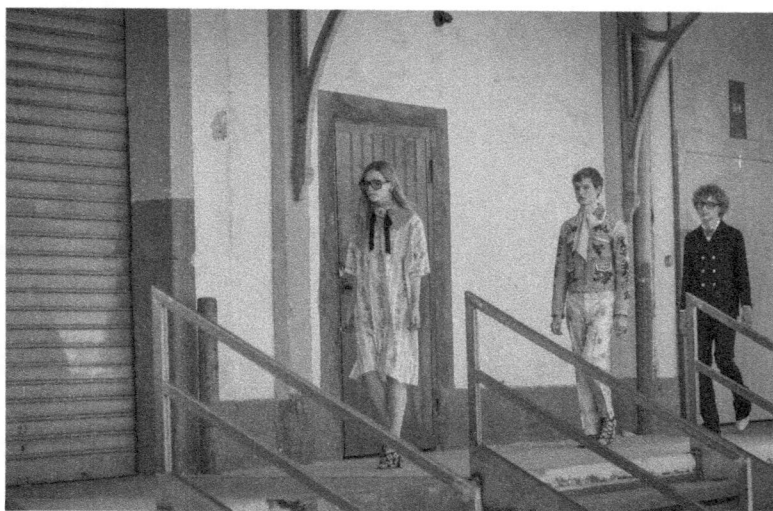

Figure 1.2. Models walking at the Gucci Spring/Summer 2016 menswear show. One model is wearing a blue leather jacket and *lavallière* blouse (Photo: taniavolobueva/Shutterstock.com).

reusing of already established and existing artistic elements into a new ensemble, a re-signification. As Gabriel Zacarias writes,

> The aim of *détournement* is not to erase the original. The element which is *détourné* acquires new meaning once it is inserted into a new semantic context. Nevertheless, the original meaning is still there, latent. *Détournement* is an operation of pluri-signification; it contains different layers of meaning. Moreover, it attains its maximum effect when the reader or spectator is able to grasp the whole sense of the operation, by recognising the original element and consequently the *détournement* of meaning which is introduced.[23]

Michele hijacks temporal and gender signifiers and re-contextualizes them, layering them with new meaning in the now: pyjama sets alongside outerwear, pussycat bows and scattered flowers alongside bleached denim and patent leather, silk brocades and studded leather, 1970s-inspired silhouettes and flared trousers alongside eighteenth-century prints and patterns. This apparent disparity works because we can read and understand these signs as coming from another time, place or (sub-)culture. It is, as Michele writes in the show notes, 'through the playful ability to grasp what already exists and combine it in a new context of meaning', that 'each fragment receives a new impulse of life'.[24]

For the Spring/Summer 2016 womenswear collection, Michele applied a similar approach inspired by a Situationist's technique: the *dérive*. Developed by members of the Letterist International, *dérive* is defined as 'A mode of experimental behavior linked to the conditions of urban society: a technique of rapid passage through varied ambiences'.[25] Rather than focussing on everyday routes and social environments, *dérive* emphasizes the unplanned journey through urban spaces, shaped and influenced by the stimuli emanating from a city. Getting lost and emotionally disoriented as a result is thus what leads to potential creation and an opportunity for learning.

In Michele's fashion design, *dérive* becomes the 'exploratory process of collecting and interpreting signs, clues, traces of life, emotional states, and symbolic worlds'.[26] The result was an amalgamation of glittering flower-embroidered satin and chiffon dresses and skirts, sparkling *trompe-l'oeil* bows and volants, Lurex knits and shining brocade and floral-pattern suits (Figure 1.3). The accessories were similarly lavishly decorated with purl-studded heels, ties with embroidered fruits and insects, large pussy bow ties and nerdy glasses with rhinestones. Many pieces and techniques from the menswear collection found their way into womenswear, the flower-embroidered and studded leather jacket, yellow silk pants or the double-G trench coat, here embellished with flower prints (Figure 1.4).

Besides the technique of the *dérive*, Madeleine de Scudéry's 1654 *Carte de Tendre*, the map of tender, was a main source of inspiration for Michele and was printed on one of the dresses (Figure 1.5). Conceived as a social game, the map is based entirely on the theme of love and tenderness, representing the path to love through villages of *Billet Doux* (love letter), *Petit Soins*

Figure 1.3. Runway look from Gucci's Spring/Summer 2016 ready-to-wear show. The model is wearing a floral print, shrunken suit (FashionStock.com/Shutterstock.com).

Figure 1.4. A model walking the runway at the Gucci Spring/ Summer 2016 ready-to-wear show, wearing a pink pussy bow blouse and embroidered leather jacket (Photo: FashionStock.com/ Shutterstock.com).

Figure 1.5. Runway look from the Gucci Spring/Summer 2016 ready-to-wear show. The model is wearing a dress with a *Carte de Tendre* print and *trompe-l'oeil* details (Photo: FashionStock.com/ Shutterstock.com).

(little trinkets), *Tendre-sur-Estime* (Tender-on-Esteem) and *Tendre-sur-Reconnaissance* (Tender-on-Recognition). In Michele's fashion world, the garments become maps capturing not only aesthetic tenderness, but feelings, emotions and references that might make you feel lost in its abundant opulence but that also offer fluid movement and identification.

The advertising campaign for the Spring/Summer 2016 collections also played with the re-contextualizing of the collections and sartorial signs. The images and video were shot in Berlin by Glen Luchford under the direction of Alessandro Michele and Christopher Simmonds and reimagined the harsh looks reminiscent of Uli Edel's movie adaptation of *Wir Kinder vom Bahnhof Zoo* (Christiane F., 1978; Engl. title: *Zoo Station: The Story of Christiane F.*) in a hazy and romantic advertising campaign. A group of young intellectuals and hippies celebrated against the backdrop of Berlin's subway stations and Karl-Marx-Allee rooftops and – seemingly carefree – played with the concepts of gender fluidity in their maximalist, eclectic and vintage-inspired looks.[27] The campaign captured Michele's characters living and getting lost in urban spaces, including the young man wearing a *lavallière* and denim shorts, riding a skateboard to work.

Gucci Fall/Winter 2016/2017

Michele's reassembling of sartorial signs and symbols also takes shape in the Fall/Winter 2016/2017 menswear collection. Rich brocades and silks were shown alongside purposefully creased suits (once again somewhat shrunken and seemingly inherited), snakeskin suits and fringed jackets, loafers and heels embedded with studs and pearls and sunglasses embellished with crystals. What is more, the models wore soft pink knitted hats with tassels and cat ears, Snoopy prints on t-shirts and flower embroideries on tailored and knitted jackets. There was also a light pink satin blouse jacket resembling the Japanese *sukajan*, also known as souvenir or tour jacket.

The *sukajan* was originally crafted and embroidered by Japanese craftsmen as a souvenir for American soldiers stationed in Occupied Japan after World War II. Modelled after American bomber or varsity jackets, they were often crafted from silk or rayon and featured a mix of Western and Eastern motives such as animals from Asian mythology (tigers, dragons) or American military insignia and iconography. This fusion of Japanese and American symbolism not only speaks to the garment's transcultural origin, but the complexity of a 'self-orientalism' employed as a marketing strategy to combat the difficult economic climate in post-war Japan. Later, the style was adopted by Japanese working-class youth culture as an act of defiance, layering its meaning with rebellion.[28] In recent years, the jacket's visibility in media and pop culture further circulated its image in the mainstream. In 2003, Tom Ford designed a *sukajan* blouson for Gucci's Spring/Summer collection, in 2011, Ryan Gosling wore a white *sukajan* with a yellow scorpion on the back for the film *Drive* (dir. Nicolas Winding Refn).

In the menswear collection, entitled 'Poetic Reactivation', the *sukajan* jacket appears alongside western fringe blazers, capes, embroidered trucker jackets, knitted grandfather vests and pussy bow shirts, jersey tracksuits embellished with art deco style patterns, and T-shirts and knitwear featuring Peanuts characters or 'Bowie' lettering. Here, it is again Michele's penchant for plundering the past and re-contextualizing its signs in a contemporary, reassembled context. In the show notes, Michele refers once more to Walter Benjamin and his concept of history and the dialectical image, writing that,

> The traces that reach us from the past are neither lifeless, petrified relics nor mere museum objects. Rather, we must understand them as sparks capable of igniting the fuse of the explosive material contained within the past. Sparks capable of creating constellations rich in futures, in which the past can meet the present.[29]

By rejecting, distorting and inverting sartorial signs of the past, the Fall/Winter 2016/2017 menswear collection 'creates unprecedented emotional palimpsests with a surplus of meaning and desire. An excess of meaningfulness that cannot be fully absorbed', but that offers a fluidity and multiplicity of garments, looks and signs in the now.[30]

The Fall/Winter 2016/2017 womenswear collection continued this plundering approach to the past and present. From Caterina de' Medici and 1970s sportwear to renaissance biker and 1980s

Italian and French couture – these are just a few keywords used to describe Michele's colourful and glittering composition for Gucci's 'Rhizomatic Scores' collection. Referring here to Gilles Deleuze and Félix Guattari's concept of the rhizome, which 'has no beginning or end; it is always in the middle, between things, interbeing, *intermezzo*',[31] Michele's collection is an exemplary accumulation of historic and cultural references. An intermezzo of nonlinear, fluid signs that scramble the notion of chronology and resist unambiguous assignment and causality: puffy 1980s shoulder details, a sequinned *cheongsam* or *qipao* with koi fish and snake prints, sixteenth-century bodices, bright yellow and pink fur coats, an evening dress looking like a sports jersey embroidered with baroque beading along the neck. Soft, see-through chiffon mixed with librarian tweed jackets and pussy bow blouses, satin skirts and jackets mixed with lush brocades and distressed leather jackets – once again, these gender-fluid pieces were worn by all genders. As Michele writes, 'Each garment brings very different sign systems into play, intertwining them in diverse and non-hierarchical directions', thus creating 'a score of references that blend, modify, and communicate with each other in unpredictable contexts of meaning'.[32]

Gucci Fall/Winter 2017/2018

The Fall/Winter 2017/2018 ready-to-wear collection was the first one following Gucci's announcement to combine its womenswear and menswear shows. Consequently, the collection consisted of a total of 119 looks, and like his previous collections, it was an amalgamation of prints, patterns and (pop) cultural references. If there was a common theme, it would be that of eclectic maximalism and botanical gardens. In the show notes, Michele describes the show as an alchemist's garden, offering a list of plants and animals that appear throughout the collection: beetles, caterpillars, moths, ladybugs, dragonflies, grasshoppers, butterflies, bees and ants are listed as well as, bats, squirrels, raccoons, cats, tigers, wolves, owls, eagles, frogs, snakes and lizards. Flowers like water lilies, roses, violets, peonies, daffodils, daisies, irises, wisteria and poppies are embroidered and printed on dresses, pants and jackets and embellish bags, shoes and other accessories like Japanese paper parasols.

However, the collection would not be Michele's collection if there were no other disparate signs commingling in and on the garments. Ski-pants were worn over a printed shirt with mice and flowers, rhinestones and crystals embroidered over checked shirts and woollen coats, patent leather pants and pleated chiffon dresses, lush lurex and satin gowns with 1980s voluminous hairstyles, sweatbands and headbands with Gucci lettering and sequins on lapel and suit jackets, sharply tailored suits and flared pants were contrasted with printed leggings, boxing shorts and boots. Punk references came in the form of studded leather jackets, ripped denim shorts and nose piercings worn by several boys and girls of Michele's tribe of unconventionally beautiful people. In line with his penchant for the past, Michele included several versions of the *lavallière* – worn once again regardless of gender –, seventeenth- and eighteenth-century chinoiserie prints, and eighteenth-century brocade knee breeches.

While the overwhelming amount of stylized botanical prints and patterns might suggest a nature inspired set for the show, instead, the models walked along a tubular walkway with steel girder on one side and plexiglass on the other, separating the models from the audience and creating 'a subliminally strange, uneasy aura', as Sarah Mower writes.[33] In the designer's words, it was an alchemist's garden 'inhabited by signs, symbols, and archetypes that conjure and summon distant worlds'. Accordingly, this alchemist's garden was an anti-modern laboratory, as Michele writes in the show notes,

> for it rejects some of the principles underlying a certain scientific approach characterized by rigidity and determinism. It is the place where the deadly logic of excluded contradiction is overcome. The place where ambivalence is celebrated, understood as the possibility of jointly accepting opposing explanations of reality. Within this framework, the dualisms of man and woman, being and appearance, light and shadow, immanence and transcendence, body and mind, good and evil, inside and outside – the classificatory approaches and rigid divisions – disappear.[34]

Michele's anti-modern and alchemist's garden was even prevalent backstage, with each look accompanied with its own decorated box for shoes, bags and jewellery. The boxes featured printed pictures of the Dutch Golden Age Old Master's still lifes of parrot tulips photoshopped with iPhone charger cables. This mix of old, classic artworks and modern technology seems to fit perfectly in Michele's world of cross-cultural and nonlinear signs. Fittingly, the invitation to the show – a vinyl record – featured an A-side of Florence Welch reciting from William Blake's collection of illustrated poems, *Songs of Innocence and of Experience* (1794), and a B-side of A$AP Rocky reading Frederick Wentworth's love letter from Jane Austen's *Persuasion* (1817).[35] The abundant use of floral and botanic prints throughout the collection was not just due to Michele's disparate alchemist's garden, but was in reference to Gucci's archive: many of the prints came from Gucci's scarf-print archives.

The use of these floral prints as well as other cultural references such as Japanese parasols, *sukajans* and *pankou* or frog closures, also speak to Western fashion's ongoing obsession with the East, with orientalism and 'exotic' ideas and aesthetics. As Jennifer Craik argues, exoticism plays an important role in the constant renewal of (Western) fashion design: 'In other words, exoticism and fashion go hand in hand such that references to cultural motifs are a foremost inspiration in fashion', creating 'narratives of difference and distinctiveness'.[36] These 'exotic' costumes are frequently used to construct identities and aesthetics that are positioned as other, foreign, and deviant in relation to Western norms, and at times even framed as potentially threatening. However, as Adam Geczy writes, contemporary floral designs exemplify the way in which orientalism has entered Western fashion 'unconsciously', where their origin has been lost, and their symbolism and aesthetic have become widespread signs in art and design.[37]

In Michele's fashion design, however, these signs and symbols are emphasized, turned upside-down, clashing with fabrics and references from other cultures and times, be that West or East, eighteenth-century court or twentieth-century punk subcultural style, haute couture or sportswear. 'This is precisely why fashion is so similar to alchemy', Michele writes, 'one combines elements of knowledge and matter, ostensibly distant and incompatible realities, only to distil an elixir that allows us to live better and more intensely'.[38]

Gucci Fall/Winter 2020/2021

When Michele introduced his new vision for Gucci by introducing his geeky, unconventional characters, it was not just the gender fluidity of the clothes, but the soft and unconventional masculinity that pervaded throughout the collection. From the very first look, the young, long-haired model in a red *lavallière* blouse, Michele challenged traditional masculinity, interrogating contemporary norms of gender through the prism of fluidity. Consequently, he envisioned forms of masculinity far away from the hyper-masculinity and the sexy hedonism of his predecessors, instead offering a collection that was 'soft power, gender-fluid, pussy-bow'ed, and *pretty*', as *Vogue* editor Luke

Leitch writes.[39] For Gucci Fall/Winter 2020/2021 menswear, Michele dedicated the collection to the renegotiation and examination of masculinity, emphasizing not only softer forms but the plurality and multiplicity of gender and masculinity.

In the show notes titled 'Masculine, Plural', Michele condemns the toxic masculinity prevalent in patriarchal society. Accordingly, masculine gender identity is shaped by harmful and oppressive stereotypes that reinforce toxic conceptions of masculinity:

> A dominant, winning, oppressive masculinity model is imposed on babies at birth. [...] Any possible reference to femininity is aggressively banned, as it is considered a threat against the complete affirmation of a masculine prototype that allows no divergencies. There is nothing natural in this drift. The model is socially and culturally built to reject anything that doesn't comply with it.[40]

While Michele does not mention them by name, it seems that he is referring here to the social constructivism of gender and Judith Butler's notion of gender performativity. According to Butler, gender is not a biological fact, but a continuously repeating activity. It is something one does, rather than something one is. Through a stylized repetition of performative acts, including the way we dress, gender is constructed while simultaneously hiding its genesis.[41] Institutions and social mechanisms regulate or punish those that strive from the norms of gender expression.

For Michele, however, fashion and masculine dress offer a way to proliferate and expand the notion of masculinity/masculinities, proposing a 'desertion, away from patriarchal plans and uniforms':

> Deconstructing the idea of masculinity as it has been historically established. [...] It's time to celebrate a man who is free to practice self-determination, without social constraints, without authoritarian sanctions, without suffocating stereotypes. A man who is able to reconnect with his core of fragility, with his trembling and his tenderness. [...] A man full of kindness and care. [...] A man who is also sister, mother, bride. [...] It's not about suggesting a new normative model, rather to release what was constrained. Breaking a symbolic order, which is nowadays useless. Nourishing a space of possibility where masculinity can shake off its toxicity, to freely regain what was taken away. And, in doing this, turning back time, learning to unlearn.[42]

This learning to unlearn takes shape in the collection as a soft, gender-fluid or antigender fashion that contrasts and mixes masculine and feminine sartorial signifiers.[43] The collection consisted of fluffy baby-pink and blue sweaters with children's book motifs, A-line dresses and coats with Peter-Pan collars, gingham and checked patterns on coats and dresses (some of which were worn over distressed and ripped jeans). A puffer jacket, several bags and Peter-Pan-collared dresses and some pairs of shoes also featured Liberty floral prints – a choice that Michele explained with his love for florals, adding that 'of course, *liberty* means freedom, so I decided to be a bit playful with this side – and it is a fantastic store, you go back to your childhood to be in it'.[44]

Childhood and its aesthetics seemed to be a central element in this collection, with many looks referencing classic school uniforms and preadolescent attire: several looks featured knickerbockers, knee-high socks with the double-G pattern, and black leather-strap sandals and shape sorter bags, while the gingham patterns and baby-doll dresses also carried a playful character. Yet, other looks referenced 1990s grunge style with oversized checked shirts and ripped denim jeans, as well as Kurt Cobain's knitted cardigans, while others featured metallic flared pants and hair-dos reminiscent of David Bowie's stage outfits. There were also T-shirts designed in collaboration with punk rocker Richard Hell, reading 'impatience' and 'impotence'. Here it is again, Michele's penchant for plundering past aesthetics and contrasting disparate signs that creates this multi-layered collection.

In other words, it is Michele's concept of nonlinear time and plurality of aesthetics and codes that creates his fluid fashion design. Emblematic of this nonlinearity was the installation for the Fall/Winter 2020/2021 show. In the centre of the runway, a big pendulum swung back and forth at first, drawing a line in the sand that covered the runway. With the start of the show, the pendulum began to swing from different angles, demonstrating both Michele's nonlinear conception of time and the nonlinearity of fashion. Michele's Gucci gang, his unconventionally beautiful boys and girls that dress in an eclectic mix of heirloom pieces, vintage shop finds, *lavallières* and floral patterns exist beyond gender, beyond time and place. As a quote by the artist Coco Capitán, scribbled on the shoe boxes and invitation for the Fall/Winter 2017/2018 show, asks, 'What are we going to do with all this future?' In Michele's world, this future will be, above all, a fluid one.

Notes

1 Gucci. 'The Future Is Fluid'. *Gucci* 2022b, accessed 31 March 2025, https://www.gucci.com/us/en/st/stories/article/chime-for-change-the-future-is-fluid-film?srsltid=AfmBOopVnREZRI9x32_5dCQwi QWQASCQZbVf8PeRjK6jbxjM14f2QgQB.

2 Jonathan Wingfield, 'The Happy Couple: Marco Bizzarri & Alessandro Michele', *System Magazine*, 2016, https://system-magazine. com/issues/issue-7/alessandro-michele-marco-bizzarri.

3 Emanuele Coccia and Alessandro Michele, *Das Leben der Formen: Eine Philosophie der Wiederverzauberung*, trans. Thomas Stauder (München: Hanser, 2025), 28, my translation.

4 Lynn Hirschberg, 'Alessandro Michele Reflects on Making a Gucci Collection in One Week', *W Magazine*, 2 February 2020, https:// www.wmagazine.com/story/gucci-alessandro-michele-interview.

5 Coccia and Michele, *Das Leben der Formen: Eine Philosophie der Wiederverzauberung*, 30.

6 Judith Beyer, *Antigender Fashion: The Possibilities of Gender-Fluid and Non-Binary Fashion Design* (London: Bloomsbury Visual Arts, 2025), 62.

7 Ingrid Loschek, *Reclams Mode- und Kostümlexikon* (Stuttgart: Reclam, 2011), 354.

8 Fleur Britten, 'Take a bow: Kate Moss outfit sends subversive message at Depp libel trial', *The Guardian*, 27 May 2022, https://www.theguardian.com/film/2022/may/27/kate-moss-outfit-johnny-depp-amber-heard-trial.

9 Adam Geczy and Vicki Karamias, 'Power + Fashion', *Foucault Studies*, no. 36 (2024): 202, https://doi.org/10.22439/fs.i36.7230.

10 Coccia and Michele, *Das Leben der Formen: Eine Philosophie der Wiederverzauberung*, 47.

11 Ibid., 32.

12 Beyer, *Antigender Fashion: The Possibilities of Gender-Fluid and Non-Binary Fashion Design*, 45–58.

13 Jack Halberstam, *Trans*: A Quick and Quirky Account of Gender Variability* (Oakland: University of California Press, 2018).

14 Hamish Bowles, 'Inside the Wild World of Gucci's Alessandro Michele', *Vogue*, 15 April 2019, https://www.vogue.com/article/gucci-alessandro-michele-interview-may-2019-issue.

15 Giorgio Agamben, 'What Is the Contemporary?', in *'What Is an Apparatus?' And Other Essays*, ed. Werner Hamacher, Meridian: Crossing Aesthetics Series (Stanford: Stanford University Press, 2009), 40–41. Original italics.

16 Ibid., 39.

17 Daniel Blanga-Gubbay, 'The Distance with the Present. On Agamben's Notion of the Contemporary', *Documenta* 34, no. 2 (2020): 90–91, https://doi.org/10.21825/doc.v34i2.16387.

18 Walter Benjamin, *The Arcades Project*, trans. Howard Eiland and Kevin McLaughlin (Cambridge, Massachuestts, and London, England: Belknap Press of Harvard University Press, 2002), 462.

19 Agamben, 'What Is the Contemporary?', 48–50.

20 Coccia and Michele, *Das Leben der Formen: Eine Philosophie der Wiederverzauberung*, 31.

21 Judith Beyer, 'Out of reach: Gucci's 'Tian' suit between material culture and gender-fluid imagination', *Clothing Cultures* 11, no. 1 (2024), https://doi.org/10.1386/cc_00079_1.

22 Guy Debord, 'Definitions', in *Situationist International Anthology*, ed. and trans. Ken Knabb (Berkeley, CA: Bureau of Public Secrets, 2006), 52.

23 Gabriel Zacarias, 'Détournement in Language and the Visual Arts', in *The Situationist International: A Critical Handbook*, ed. Alastair Hemmens and Gabriel Zacarias (London: Pluto Press, 2020), 218. Original italics.

24 Coccia and Michele, *Das Leben der Formen: Eine Philosophie der Wiederverzauberung*, 195.

25 Debord, 'Definitions', 52.

26 Coccia and Michele, *Das Leben der Formen: Eine Philosophie der Wiederverzauberung*, 197.

27 Judith Beyer, 'Beyond the Binary: A Close Reading of Gender-Fluid Masculinities in Gucci's Spring/Summer 2016 Campaign', *Journal of Bodies, Sexualities, and Masculinities* 4, no. 1 (2023), https://doi.org/10.3167/jbsm.2023.040108.

28 Sarah Cheang, Erica de Greef, and Yoko Takagi, *Rethinking Fashion Globalization* (London: Bloombury Visual Arts, 2021), 50; Elizabeth Kramer, 'New vintage – new history? The sukajan (souvenir jacket) and its fashionable reproduction', *International Journal of Fashion Studies* 7, no. 1 (2020), https://doi.org/10.1386/infs_00015_1.

29 Coccia and Michele, *Das Leben der Formen: Eine Philosophie der Wiederverzauberung*, 199.

30 Ibid., 200.

31 Gilles Deleuze and Félix Guattari, *A Thousand Plateaus: Capitalism and Schizophrenia* (London and New York: Continuum, 2004), 27.

32 Coccia and Michele, *Das Leben der Formen: Eine Philosophie der Wiederverzauberung*, 202.

33 Sarah Mower, 'Gucci Fall 2017 Ready-To-Wear', *Vogue*, 22 Feburary 2017, https://www.vogue.com/fashion-shows/fall-2017-ready-to-wear/gucci.

34 Coccia and Michele, *Das Leben der Formen: Eine Philosophie der Wiederverzauberung*, 207–09.

35 Mower, 'Gucci Fall 2017 Ready-To-Wear'.

36 Jennifer Craik, 'Exotic Narratives in Fashion: The Impact of Motifs
    of Exotica on Fashion Design and Fashionable Identities', in *Modern
    Fashion Traditions: Negotiating Tradition and Modernity through Fashion*,
    ed. M. Angela Jansen and Jennifer Craik (London: Bloomsbury
    Academic, 2018), 98.

37 Adam Geczy, *Fashion and Orientalism: Dress, Textiles and Culture from the
    17th to the 21st Century* (London: Bloomsbury Academic, 2013), 7.

38 Coccia and Michele, *Das Leben der Formen: Eine Philosophie der
    Wiederverzauberung*, 31.

39 Luke Leitch, 'Gucci Fall 2020 Menswear', *Vogue*, 14 January 2020,
    https://www.vogue.com/fashion-shows/fall-2020-menswear/gucci.

40 Coccia and Michele, *Das Leben der Formen: Eine Philosophie der
    Wiederverzauberung*, 225.

41 Judith Butler, *Gender Trouble: Feminism and the Subversion of Identity* (New
    York: Routledge, 2006).

42 Coccia and Michele, *Das Leben der Formen: Eine Philosophie der
    Wiederverzauberung*, 226.

43 Beyer, *Antigender Fashion: The Possibilities of Gender-Fluid and Non-Binary
    Fashion Design*, 129.

44 Luke Leitch, 'Gucci Fall 2020 Menswear', *Vogue*, 14 January 2020,
    https://www.vogue.com/fashion-shows/fall-2020-menswear/gucci.

Chapter 2

BIZARRE BEAUTY

Fashion and beauty are in many ways inextricably linked – just look at any fashion magazine and their multi-page spreads on beauty, make-up and fragrances. As Brian Moeran writes, 'beauty is an essential part of *The Look* that every serious fashion magazine reader should aspire to'.[1] Beyond that, fashion and beauty have long played an important and visible part in reinforcing cultural systems, each participating in the articulation of the idealized body, desire and the aesthetics of contemporary times. Beauty, as neither a neutral nor timeless category, is deeply embedded in the cultural zeitgeist – it reflects prevailing values, anxieties and ideas surrounding gender, race, class, and sexuality. Fashion, in turn, does not merely reflect these ideals but actively produces, distorts and disseminates them. What is deemed beautiful – or desirable – is thus in a constant state of negotiation, shaped by shifting historical, social and political forces.

As Umberto Eco emphasizes in *The History of Beauty* (2004), beauty is not a fixed or universal ideal, but a historically and culturally constructed concept that has evolved over time in tandem with shifting philosophical, religious and aesthetic paradigms, and which to this day is strongly influenced by a Eurocentric colonial gaze. By mapping out a genealogy of beauty in Western culture, Eco presents beauty as always tied to the cultural and theoretical frameworks of the time. In classical antiquity, for instance, beauty was often associated with harmony, proportion and mathematical order – exemplified in Ancient Greek sculpture, architecture and Platonic and Aristotelian philosophy. In medieval times, beauty became aligned with the divine, while by the time of the renaissance, beauty returned to a more human-centred ideal, rooted in anatomical precision and the revival of classical harmony and proportions. Yet, at the same time, beauty in the Renaissance and throughout much of its history is also tinged with contradicting, unsettling forces that lead to a multiplicity of beauty. In other words, beauty is not merely what pleases the eyes, but also what provokes thought, desire, and even discomfort.

During the Romantic period in particular, beauty gained another level of meaning. With its emphasis on emotion, imagination and individual experiences in contrast to reason and logic, the Romantic movement understood beauty no longer as solely harmonious, idealized or classically balanced. Instead, Romanticism embraced the emotional, the melancholic, the grotesque and the irrational – ushering in a notion of a tainted beauty that does not try to exclude contradictions but to dissolve them in a common presence.[2] Beauty became bound not to form or perfection, but to intensity of feeling and included concepts of darkness and excess, often intertwined with themes of longing, nostalgia and death. This fatal concept of Romantic beauty becomes apparent in Victor Hugo's 1872 sonnet, *Ave, dea; moriturus te salutat*, in which he writes: 'Death and beauty are two things profound / So of dark and azure, that one might say that / They were two sisters terrible and fecund / Possessing the one enigma, the one secret'.[3]

This Romantic redefinition of beauty as imperfect, elusive and emotionally charged finds a striking contemporary echo in Alessandro Michele's work, whose collections have often been described as romantic. Michele has consistently drawn on Romantic sensibilities – aesthetically and philosophically – to shape a vision of fashion that is rich in historical reference, poetic ambiguity and bizarre beauty. His designs often evoke a sense of temporal dislocation, layering elements from Victorian-style dresses, ecclesiastical garments and baroque ornamentation with contemporary streetwear and camp irony. This collage-like approach mirrors the Romantic fascination with ruins, the ugly and grotesque. As Vicki Karaminas and Justine Taylor write, Michele's 'Gucci became synonymous with the unconventional: the ugly became beautiful, imperfection became perfection, and the undesirable became desirable'.[4]

Gucci Cruise 2019

Michele's recurring engagement with themes of beauty, death, and the uncanny resonates deeply with the Romantic imagination, in which beauty and mortality are inseparable.

Just as the Romantics saw beauty in the ephemeral and the mournful, Michele often constructs an aesthetic that is at once tender and macabre, nostalgic and visionary, and that is infused with mythological and historical references. This contradictory embrace of beauty was perhaps most vividly staged in the Gucci Cruise 2019 collection show held in the Alyscamps outside the old town walls of Arles in the south of France.

The Roman necropolis was one of the most famous necropolizes of the ancient world. Its name derives from the Provençal Occitan word *Aliscamps*, which in turn stems from the Latin *Elisii Campi* – a term referring to the Elysian Fields, or the *Champs-Élysées* in French, the mythological paradise reserved for the blessed in Greco-Roman tradition. The site's associations with death, transcendence, and the afterlife do not end there. Referenced in literary works such as Ariosto's *Orlando Furioso* and Dante's *Inferno*, the Alyscamps serve as a symbolic space tied to memory, loss and the passage between worlds.

In Michele's phantasmagorical world, the necropolis becomes the scene for his time-travelling, iconoclastic characters, his 'widows attending grave sites, kids playing rock 'n' roll stars, and ladies who aren't ladies'.[5] Dressed in toga-like dresses and Victorian-inspired gowns, sharply flared 1970s pantsuits and Chanel-style jackets, Michele's models walked alongside a line of fire in the middle of the walkway. Holding funeral bouquets, Michele's tribe of unconventional beautiful people entered the runway through the Medieval Church of Saint Honoratus, emphasizing the ritualistic and elysian atmosphere of the space. 'Alyscamps is not what it seems', Michele said, 'Alyscamps is a Roman cemetery, but it's not a cemetery; it was a promenade, then it became a walk in 1700 – it is a hybrid place which has several significances'.[6]

Michele's designs echoed the multi-layered meaning and references of this place. He invoked regional traditions with nods to the traditional dress of the Camargue and the Arlésienne, blending folkloric elements with high fashion ornamentation. English checked tweeds appeared alongside shimmering tinsel fringe, collegiate sportswear mingled with matador references and accessories (scarves, oversized glasses, elaborate headpieces) completed each look with a sense of exaggerated, almost devotional stylization: Heavy, bejewelled crosses accompanied every other look, worn around the neck or held in the hand like a rosary. Among the most memorable pieces was a black velvet gown with an intricately embroidered golden skeleton thorax adorning the bodice – a *memento mori*. This motif recurred throughout the collection, with the phrase scribbled across the legs on skin-tight leggings. Other references to the inevitability of death came in the form of jewellery reminiscent of medieval graves, and floral prints resembling baroque *Vanitas* still lifes. In this way, Michele summoned both religious iconography and gothic theatricality staged against the backdrop of the necropolis.

As Caroline Evans writes in *Fashion at the Edge* (2003), much of fashion history, and particularly the high-end luxury and avant-garde designers at the end of the twentieth century, including

Alexander McQueen and Martin Margiela, is filled with *memento mori* and themes of horror, decay, death and mortality. As Evans writes, fashion 'turns out to be shot through with alienation and melancholy, which are always threatening to erupt and disturb the smoothness of its surface'.[7] In other words, fashion loves to play with death, with the allure of beauty inflicted with horror – a defining feature of the woman of fashion as Walter Benjamin writes, who Michele references frequently. Accordingly,

> fashion was never anything but the parody of the gaily decked-out corpse, the provocation of death through the woman, and (in between noisy, canned slogans) the bitter, whispered *tête-à-tête* with decay. That is fashion. For this reason she changes so rapidly, teasing death, already becoming something else again, something new, as death looks about for her in order to strike her down.[8]

In Michele's fashion design, death becomes a place of metamorphoses, of rebirth, of resurrection and immortality. Though he references themes of death and decay, in line with Michele's temporal dislocations and nonlinearity of time and history, nothing is truly dead. Rather, his collections are full of vitality, equipped with signs and symbols once forgotten, waiting to be mixed and combined with contemporary, post-postmodern and pop-cultural references. This is particularly apparent in the advertising campaign for the Gucci Spring/ Summer 2018 collection. Illustrated by Spanish artist Ignasi

Monreal, the so-called 'Gucci Hallucination' campaign featured a compilation of classic artworks re-imagined with Michele's otherworldly, eclectic designs. At the end of the video campaign, Monreal, playing the curator walking us through the illustrations, steps into one of his re-works: a lily covered pond inspired by John Everett Millais' *Ophelia* (1852). Here, it is not just the illustration that becomes alive, but the model/Ophelia herself as Monreal helps 'the tragic beauty dressed in Alessandro Michele's gold sequinned dress out of her watery grave'.[9]

Gucci 'Cyborg', Fall/Winter 2018/2019

In no other collection is Michele's design approach to an uncanny, bizarre beauty as evident as in the Gucci Fall/Winter 2018/2019 collection, the Cyborg collection. Held in February 2018, the Gucci Hub in Milan was reimagined as a clinical operating theatre, including emergency exits, operating tables and surgical light heads. The space was dominated by block-panelled walls in a muted surgical green, echoing the colour of medical scrubs (as a complementary colour to (blood) red, it offers high contrast and avoids visual fatigue). At the centre of the runway, two parallel operating tables – draped in matching green fabric – were positioned on a square of stark red linoleum, creating an eerie reminder of the potential blood loss in surgery. The remainder of the floor, along with the ceiling, was coated in a pale blue, interrupted only by white LED strips and intense surgical lights suspended above the beds. This harsh, utilitarian lighting, combined with the sterile materials, produced a charged and unsettling atmosphere that was only heightened by the beeping sound of a heart monitor and the inhaling sounds of a ventilator at the beginning of the show. Surrounding the set were rows of plastic chairs, often found in hospital waiting rooms, repurposed here not for patients but for an audience bearing witness to Michele's fashion operation: 'There's a clinical clarity about what I am doing', Michele said, 'I was thinking of a space that represents the creative act. I wanted to represent the lab I have in my head. It's physical work, like a surgeon's'.[10]

The installation for the Fall/Winter 2018/2019 collection, with its clinical and spare aesthetic, did not leave 'much room for everyday insinuations of beauty and pleasure'. Rather, Gucci's spectacle of the fashion chamber, as Adam Geczy and Vicki Karaminas write, offers its spectators 'something that has been hidden, even forbidden', creating an uncanny (*unheimlich*) atmosphere in which Michele's posthuman models paraded in an eclectic mix of hybrid designs of a temporal and cultural elsewhere.[11] While the Gucci Cyborg collection has been described as a space or chamber of horrors sealed off from the everyday, or as a show of provocation to envision 'an obligatory worlding and new social order', it primarily speaks to Michele's idiosyncratic, uncanny, postgender and posthuman imaginings.[12]

The clothes, borrowed, appropriated and reconfigured, operated as visual assemblages – fragments of time, cultures and genres spliced together to form strange, and at times unsettling compositions. Ranging from traditionally tailored suits to elaborate folkloric dresses, medieval-inspired tunics and garments suggestive of ecclesiastical or ceremonial dress, the designs juxtaposed and recontextualized disparate signs in intentional clashing of references: pagoda shoulders appeared next to 1980s-style prom dresses; Renaissance florals clashed with synthetic fabrics; the logo of New York Yankees baseball team was embroidered on garments like hound tooth coats, lace trimmed blouses and woollen beanies; and Russ Meyer's 1965 *Faster, Pussycat! Kill! Kill!* movie title graphic appeared on a sweater worn with a long shirt, checkered pants and rhinestone balaclava. Intricate embroidery, metallic thread, brocade, lace, sequins and crystal appliqués adorned many of the pieces, often interrupting or obscuring traditional garment structures. Michele's maximalism was on full display: garments layered atop garments, mismatched prints and patterns in an intentional defiance of minimalism or restraint. Accessories heightened this eclectic mix: there were oversized glasses, studded balaclavas, jewel-encrusted headpieces and knitted pattern-hats.

In addition to the number of pop-cultural references and sartorial remixing, Michele conflated global cultural signifiers: Sikh turbans, Chinese cheongsams, Russian babushka scarves, Sami-style jackets and American collegiate sweatshirts all appeared, recombined with the logic of collage rather than coherence. The turban hats worn in combination with a tweed jacket, red leather pants and

Art Deco body jewellery by four Caucasian models drew critique from the Sikh community, for whom the turban is not a hat accessory but an important spiritual symbol. Later in 2019, Gucci also had to remove a polo-neck jumper that referenced a balaclava from the Cyborg collection resembling blackface minstrel make-up. As Paul Jobling, Philippa Newsbitt and Angelene Wong write, Gucci's coopting of other cultural and ethnological phenomena exemplifies the way fashion appropriates and plagiarizes cultural symbols and signs 'in the name of global(ized) fashion by seizing "authorial identity, control and capital away from the source community"'.[13]

Besides the critique voiced against Gucci's coopting and appropriation of cultural signifiers, what stood out most from the Cyborg collection was Michele's visceral embrace of the uncanny. It was not just the catwalk's medical-theatre setting that leaves the viewer with an uneasy feeling, but some of the accessories worn by the models: Several models walked the runway carrying replicas of their own heads (Figure 2.1) – a reference to the cephalophore saints depicted with severed heads in Christian art – while others appeared with eyes on the back of their hands or in the middle of their foreheads, goat horns growing from the head or cradling a baby dragon, a snake or an iguana. The prosthetic props were created by the visual and special effects studio Makinarium in Cinecittà in Rome. Once again, Michele makes use of cinematic effects to create his own specific (fashion) universe. As Leonardo Cruciano

Figure 2.1. A model walking the runway at the Gucci Fall/Winter 2018/2019 show holding a replica of their own head. (Photo: Matteo Bazzi/EPA-EFE/Shutterstock).

states, Michele 'had very precise ideas about what he wanted to achieve. [...] a fantasy so intense'.[14]

This intense fantasy was the most vivid incorporation of Donna J. Haraway's influential essay 'A Cyborg Manifesto' (1985), echoing the theme of the cyborg as a being that defies binaries and blurs the lines between human, machine and animal. Haraway developed the concept of the cyborg as a critique against traditional, essentialist notions of feminism and womanhood. As Haraway suggests, the cyborg represents the plasticity of identity, existing in-between and in resistance of binaries of human/animal, organism/machine and male/

female. In other words, the cyborg disrupts essentialist ideas of gender and biology and represents a postgender, posthuman identity that resists fixed categories of sex and gender offering new ways of thinking about embodiment, power and agency.

The Gucci Fall/Winter 2018/2019 collection, as Michele writes in the show notes, 'takes the shape of a genuine Cyborg Manifest (D. J. Haraway), in which the hybrid is metaphorically praised as a figure that can overcome the dualism and dichotomy of identity'.[15] Identity, in Michele's pluriverse, is a process of becoming, continuously developing new forms of being, of co-existence and companionship between human and animal. In Michele's own words, the cyborg

is a paradoxical creature keeping together nature and culture, masculine and feminine, normal and alien, psyche and matter. Conflicting with any category grid, the Cyborg is the expression that blends different evolving identities. Hybrid and shifting identities, built on multiple belongings, that transgress the normative discipline.[16]

It is precisely the visualization of these hybrid, shifting forms of identity that creates the collection's uncanny impression. The uncanny (German: *das Unheimliche*) refers to a psychological and aesthetic experience marked by a feeling of discomfort, eeriness, or cognitive dissonance. It arises when something is simultaneously familiar and unfamiliar. German psychiatrist Ernst Jentsch defined the uncanny in his 1906 essay 'On the

Psychology of the Uncanny' as that which causes intellectual uncertainty – particularly in situations where one struggles to determine whether something is animate or inanimate, real or artificial. He famously cited the example of the automaton Olimpia from E.T.A. Hoffmann's short story 'The Sandman' (1816) as an example. The automaton is uncanny because the boundaries between the self and the other, the living and the dead, the organic and the mechanical, become dangerously unstable.

The uncanny in Michele's surgical fashion theatre occupies a similarly dangerous space – it unsettles because it destabilizes binary categories of human and animal, male and female and plays with the familiar and unfamiliar spaces of the fashion show and operation room, calling into question the meaning of the symbolic sartorial order. As Jobling, Nesbitt and Wang write, 'the anachronistic mixing of styles in Michele's 'Cyborg' collection portends a more universal post-symbolic order [...] one in which creatures, both human and posthuman, will inhabit a future postgender pluriverse'.[17] Or, in Michele's own words, the 'Gucci Cyborg is posthuman':

it has eyes on its hands, faun horns, dragon's puppies and doubling heads. It's a biologically indefinite and culturally aware creature. The last and extreme sign of a mongrel identity under constant transformation. The symbol of an emancipatory possibility through which we can decide to become what we are.[18]

In Michele's world, fashion becomes more than a tool or instrument to express an identity. Fashion becomes an operating table, where we can create ourselves and extend our own anatomical form to regenerate new and fluid forms. As Haraway writes, 'We require regeneration, not rebirth, and the possibilities for our reconstitution include the utopian dream of the hope for a monstrous world without gender'.[19]

In extending and escaping bodily borders, Michele's designs also embodies a form of the grotesque body, or, as Patrizia Calefato writes, the body 'in the grotesque sense of a "clothed body", where covering is a carnivalesque protuberance, a parodic second skin, open without delimitations or boundaries'.[20] The grotesque body, as Mikhail Bakhtin theorized, centres around ideas of reversal, unsettling ruptures of bodily borders and transgressions. In other words, the grotesque body

is a body in the act of becoming. It is never finished, never completed; it is continually built, created, and builds and creates another body. [...] This the artistic logic of the grotesque image ignores the closed, smooth, and impenetrable surface of the body and retains only its excrescences (sprouts, buds) and orifices, only, that which leads beyond the body's limited space or into the body's depths.[21]

With the eyes on its hand, the horns on its head, the dragon puppy and the doubling head in its arms, the Gucci Cyborg 'ignores the closed, smooth and impenetrable surface of the body', leading instead 'beyond the body's limited space' and into a posthuman pluriverse.

Gucci Fall/Winter 2019/2020

For the Fall/Winter 2019/2020 Gucci collection, Michele evoked another stylistic device of the grotesque body and the carnival: the mask. Held in February 2019, the show consisted of 87 looks in total, with almost every look featuring some kind of face covering or accessory. Large sunglasses, wide-brim hats pulled down over models' faces and large colourful sun visors were included in the collection. In addition to rhinestone string curtains, artificial teardrops, collars with long spikes and metal ear coverings inspired by Eduardo Costa's gold work *Fashion Fiction I* (1966) published in the February 1968 issue of American *Vogue*.

What stood out most in the collection were the numerous masks partially and fully concealing the model's faces. While the masks were not made for sale – the rows of 5-cm long spikes would make them difficult to wear off the runway – they were the core inspiration and starting point. As Michele writes in the show notes, it is the ambiguity of the mask, its tension between display or concealment, vanity or modesty, that 'offers the opportunity to reclaim the creative roots of our existence in the world'.[22] Michele refers here to Hannah Arendt's conception of plurality and the human condition, in particular the Arendtian

plurality that signifies the potential of each human being
to achieve a sense of individuality and equality with others.
Human existence and action are intersubjective as 'men, not
Man, [*sic*] live on the earth and inhabit the world'.[23]

As Michele writes, the mask is the persona with which we
present ourselves to the world; it is a form that offers refuge and
concealment and, at the same time, exposes something hidden:
'In the mask, depth coincides with the surface. Its wearer clothes
themselves with that which exposes them'.[24] The masks created
for the show play with this duality, concealing some parts and
exposing others: Several black masks covered the upper half
of the face, embellished with long spikes along the middle and
sides of the face; a few masks in light blue, black or white had
long pointed ends along the cheeks and jawline; masks rendered
in gold metal covered one side of the face and the eye while
others looked like brass eagles with talons clutching the jawline
(Figure 2.2). The most disturbing masks, however, were those
that covered the whole face. Created in bright white, cream,
light blue and vibrant red and green, they also covered the
mouth and only left small holes for the eyes (Figure 2.3).

The latter masks in particular evoke associations with the
masks worn at the Venetian carnival. Known as the *volto*,
meaning 'face' in English, or *lava*, meaning 'ghost', this mask
is one of the most recognizable masks of the modern Venetian
Carnival. Traditionally crafted from white leather, it is often
gilded or decorated with embellishments. Unlike many other
traditional Venetian masks, the *volto* covers the full face,

Figure 2.2. A model walks the runway at the Gucci Fall/Winter 2019/2020 show wearing a golden mask covering their eye and a collar and harness with long spikes. (Photo: FashionStock.com/ Shutterstock.com).

Figure 2.3. Runway look from the Gucci Fall/Winter 2019/2020 show. The model is wearing a mask covering the whole face. (Photo: FashionStock.com/Shutterstock.com).

extending from the top of the forehead down to the entire chin, and laterally just before the ears.[25] While the so-called *baúta* mask or the plague doctor mask can be considered more traditional pieces of grotesque art, characterized by their over-emphasized nose or projecting chin, the *volto* includes simple facial features such as a sculpted nose and closed lips, offering a neutral expression. Yet, it lacks any functional mobility: the mouth is sealed, and unlike comedic masks that occasionally feature hinged jaws for speech or performance, the *volto* is entirely static, evoking a spectral, ghostly and – as is also the case in Gucci's Fall/Winter 2019/2020 collection – an uncanny presence.

In line with the carnivalesque associations of the mask, the clothes and runway show were a theatrical pageant of sartorial codes and contrasts. Michele's penchant for hybridity and fluid signs manifested in garments that collided temporal references, silhouettes, and sub- and pop-cultural markers. The collection, ranging from razor-sharp tailoring, unfinished seams and edges to oversized streetwear presented the body as a site of continuous transformation – concealed, exposed, layered and exaggerated.

Echoes of 1940s tailoring emerged as high-waisted suit trousers with wide legs cinched at the ankle and strong-shouldered blazers with nipped waists. Many of the tailored pieces were left unfinished with open seams, raw edges and basting stitches along the seams and lapels. 'Grandfather' knitwear with check patterns and floral-patterned smocks reminiscent of 1950s apron

Figure 2.4. A model walking down the runway at the Gucci Fall/ Winter 2019/2020 show, wearing a red mask, houndstooth overall and jabot. (Photo: FashionStock.com/Shutterstock.com).

dresses were juxtaposed with shimmering lurex textiles and delicate lace details, including sixteenth-century ruffs, *lavallière*, and jabot (Figure 2.4). The jabot is a lace or linen ruffle, sewn on one or both sides around the chest neckline of a men's shirt and was popular during the eighteenth century. At the end of the nineteenth century, the jabot was appropriated into womenswear and worn as a form of waterfall made of lace or chiffon almost reaching the waist.[26] In Michele's collection, the juxtaposition of classic sartorial structure with whimsical, often anachronistic accessories established a visual tension that mirrored the mask's duality – revealing through distortion.

This plurality of signifiers and carnivalesque excess continued with Michele's eclectic embrace of a multitude of references: hip-hop aesthetics in the form of oversized T-shirts, wide-leg trousers and bulky sneakers – some were not even worn but carried by hand. Out-of-place roller-skate knee pads stood in contrast to 1980s glam rock styles and silhouettes reminiscent of British rock star David Bowie's stage costumes and hair style. The subcultural layering continued further in rich floral prints, detailed embroidery and delicate lace frills in contrast to luxurious leather pieces and clashing patterns, including harlequin diamonds, houndstooth and check patterns (Figure 2.5).

While most of Michele's collections are a motley mix of colours and patterns, the Gucci Fall/Winter 2019/2020 seemed to follow a more structured sequence. A mix of yellow and brown tones were followed by dark greys and blues, which turned into yellows and greens, black and white and later

Figure 2.5. Runway look from the Gucci Fall/Winter 2019/2020 show. The model is wearing a pattern-clashing ensemble and a blue mask with spikes. (Photo: FashionStock.com/Shutterstock.com).

cream and beige. A sequence of vibrant red ensembles made from leather and wool with fur trims in the middle of the show heightened the sense of chromatic and dramatic composition. Ultimately, the Fall/Winter 2019/2020 collection was a carnivalesque procession of identities in flux, each look a disguise and a revelation. Just as the mask complicates the boundary between self and performance, these garments refused singularity – offering instead a multiplicity of selves, historical codes and aesthetic references. In this way, Michele's runway became not just a display of fashion, but a carnivalesque meditation on the hybridity and plurality of identity and the liberating potential of fashion and artifice. A meditation that fits well with Michele's conception of beauty and ambiguity. Accordingly, beauty for Michele, is ambiguous: It is not a 'static quality, but a force, namely the ability to make other existences one's own, to absorb the fates of others, to rediscover in one's own body sensations and faces that we thought were far removed'.[27]

It seems only fitting, then, that the invitation to the show came in the form of a cast of a mask of the face of Hermaphroditus. The mask was packaged like an antique statue or loan from a museum for antique art, placed in a wooden box and laid upon wood shavings with the invitation information written on the backside like an archival card. As Michele writes, the mask 'concealed within itself the secret of being and appearance, of ambiguity, of the unknown self that emerges from a distant world'.[28] In Greek mythology, Hermaphroditus was the child of Hermes and Aphrodite and, born as a boy, renowned for his extraordinary beauty. According to Ovid's *Metamorphoses*, the water nymph Salmacis fell in love with him and pleaded with the gods to be united with him forever. In response to her prayer, the gods fused their bodies into one androgynous form, resulting in the being known as Hermaphroditus – possessing both male and female physical traits.

Gucci 'Cosmogonie', Cruise 2023

While Michele's Gucci is known for its ambiguous and gender-fluid approach to fashion, the invitations to its shows are similarly infamous and sought after amongst fashion industry insiders. Besides the invitation of the Hermaphroditus mask, or the vinyl record for the Gucci Fall/Winter 2017/2018 show, there was the invitation for the Fall/Winter 2018/2019 'Cyborg' show that came in the form of an orange countdown timer with red digital numbers, enclosed in a Ziploc bag. One side of the timer displayed a 'Parental Advisory, Explicit Content' warning, while the other side listed the event details, indicating the show's potentially disturbing character as well as creating suspense and mystery.

For the Gucci Cruise 2023 entitled 'Cosmogonie', the invitation was a star – a real star that the fashion house adopted and registered in the name of the guest. The cosmological connection was in reference to the place of the show, the Castel del Monte in Puglia, Italy. Constructed between 1240 and 1250, the medieval castle is an octagonal building with eight octagonal towers, an architectural linkage to the mystical meaning of the number eight. The soundtrack of the show featured recordings of radio reports of the moon landing accompanied by cello sounds and electronic basses. Besides the references to the moon landing and the mythology of the castle, at the end of the show, the castle was also enveloped into a projected illustration of a starry firmament. The stars, which at first appeared scattered, started to move into astronomical constellations such as Virgo, Andromeda or Ara.

Those constellations, and more broadly the concept of the constellation, was the second metaphor and conceptual framework for the Cruise 2023 collection. As Michele writes, the show's connection to the cosmos and constellations was more than 'aestheticizing posturing or insubstantial decoration. For me, the concept of the constellation served to make visible how my clothing design occurs within a relationship to the past renewed through constant references and quotations'.[29] Yet again, Michele found inspiration in the writings of German philosopher Walter Benjamin, and in Hannah Arendt's descriptions of Benjamin's way of thinking. In 'The Pearl Diver', the third section of Arendt's 1968 essay on Walter Benjamin, she employs the metaphor of 'pearl diving' – a reference to William Shakespeare's *The Tempest* (1611) – to characterize Benjamin's approach to collecting and reassembling quotations. Accordingly, she attributes Benjamin the 'gift of thinking poetically'. This thinking, as Arendt writes, fed by the present, works with the 'thought fragments' it can rest from the past and gather about itself. Like a pearl diver who descends to the bottom of the sea, not to excavate the bottom and bring it to light but to pry loose the rich and the strange, the pearls and the coral in the depths, and to carry them to the surface, this thinking delves into the depths of the past – but not in order to resuscitate it the way it was and to contribute to the renewal of extinct ages.[30]

As Arendt suggests, Benjamin's mode of thought is driven by the belief that, while all living things inevitably die and decay, this process also allows for transformation. In this view, what sinks to the depths of the sea – to the depths of time – may undergo a kind of crystallization, a metamorphosis into enduring forms that resist the elements and erosion. These fragments of the past seem to await a future thinker, a 'pearl diver', who will retrieve them and reintroduce them into the present as fragments of thought, rich and strange.[31]

It was this diving for pearls of the past that drew Michele to Benjamin and his concept of the constellation, or the dialectical image. As Benjamin writes, and Michele quotes in the accompanying Gucci Cruise 2023 show notes: 'It's not that what is past casts its light on what is present, or what is present its light on what is past; rather, image is that wherein what has been comes together in a flash with the now to form a constellation'.[32] Michele's fashion design also aims to traverse this temporal, dialectical image, finding and retrieving 'pearls' of the past into the present. For fashion, as Michele writes, is 'nothing other than this search for the pearls of the cosmos, this ability to string them together and create luminous constellations that allow us, even if only for a brief moment, to feel at one with our present'.[33]

In Gucci's Cruise 2023 collection, these constellations were turned into a surrealist spectacle, a visual exploration of bodily fragmentation, theatrical excess, and chromatic dissonance that fostered Michele's aesthetic auteurism into an expressive, but refined terrain. Occupying a space between carnivalesque costumes, sharp tailoring and glamorous embellishment, the collection offered a dreamscape of distorted silhouettes and hypnotic pattern play. A key visual motif throughout the collection was the creation of disembodied figures. Garments were deliberately constructed to obscure, hide or destabilize the body's form. Fur coats, jackets and capes dramatically extended the shoulders and bodily borders and truncated the arms, producing a silhouette where limbs appeared suspended and detached from the rest of the body. Bright, shiny latex gloves were visually cut off at the fingers and reached into the upper garments, evoking the impression of corporeal incompleteness, of alien or artificial interference. The sartorial manipulation of the corporeal rendered the body itself a site of visual slippage, of fragments of something that is, at once, present and absent. This alien distortion was further emphasized by the eyewear worn by the models. Alien-esque, sculptural, white-brimmed sunglasses distorted and transformed the model's faces, evoking the aesthetic of science fiction and futuristic imaginings. These accessories contributed to the collection's overall impression of temporal and bodily dislocations and added to Michele's recurring theme of posthuman and postgender bodies.

Michele's penchant for the theatrical and carnivalesque was also evident through the references to clowning and *commedia dell'arte*, particularly in the ruff collars that encircled the necks of models and, visually, beheaded them or cut off the hands when worn around the wrist. These ruffled neckpieces, worn with fur coats to lace dresses and deep necklines, produced constellation between the past, the comedic and postmodern sensibilities. The allusion to the Harlequin continued with the inclusion of jester pants and garments bearing diamond-patterned prints, linking the collection to the historic traditions of costume, theatre and performance whilst obscuring them with its mix of glittering embellishments and sharp tailoring.

A significant hallmark of the collection was its bold and almost disorienting use of colour and pattern. Garments featured hypnotic swirls, optical stripes and clashing chromatic compositions – juxtaposing electric blues, acid greens, fiery reds and saturated purples. These visual elements defied harmony, favouring instead a vibrant and surreal aesthetic that resisted the logic of minimalist restraint. Yet, many of the individual looks offered a more refined and simplified aesthetic than previous ones. While Michele's past collections were characterized by its iconoclastic mix of disparate signs, the Cruise 2023 collection seemed more cohesive. As Michele stated:

> Clothes are mediums, strata of languages. Today, 'making fashion' doesn't mean just being a tailor, or chronicling just a one-dimensional narration. Putting together a collection has to do with talking about your idea of the world, because fashion is deeply connected to life and to humanity. [...] It's about life, it speaks a multitude of idioms, it's like a huge choir from which nobody has to be excluded.[34]

By interweaving elements of the surreal and the carnivalesque, the Gucci Cruise 2023 collection functioned as a performative disruption of fashion and beauty norms. It evoked not only the historical costumes of theatrical traditions but also the alienating aesthetics of the science fiction genre. As with much of Michele's work, the collection refused linearity or a singular reference, instead, offering a combination of signifiers through which bodies could be reimagined, obscured, or even momentarily and partially erased.

Gucci 'Twinsburg', Spring/Summer 2023

While the main purpose of the fashion show is the promotion of the industry and the selling of merchandise, in recent years, it has also become 'increasingly attuned with the spectacle, the acceleration of fashion, the expansion of digital media and the creation of extraordinary settings'. As Tiziana Ferrero-Regis and Marissa Lindquist write, the fashion show is also a multilayered and complex 'encounter between space, fashion, and the body'.[35] For Michele, the fashion show is not only a ceremonial ritual (Gucci Fall/Winter 2020/2021), or a chamber of horrors and posthuman imaginings (Gucci Fall/Winter 2018/2019), but a space for the exploration of the body and identity.

In the case of Gucci's Spring/Summer 2023 show, held in September 2022 and constituting Michele's last collection for the Italian fashion house, it was a meditation on multiplicities, identity and otherness. Titled 'Twinsburg', the show was dedicated to Michele's twin mothers, Mamma Eralda and Mamma Giuliana, as he writes, two women whose twinhood was essential for their existence and who 'magically mirrored' each other, one multiplying the other, creating a world 'where everything was double'.[36] The title of the show is a reference to the eponymous town in Ohio where, since 1976, the Twins Days take place annually on a weekend in August, celebrating thousands of identically dressed twins.

The theme of twins and of duplication is threaded throughout the collection and its staging. The interior walls of the room were covered with large photographs depicting the model's faces. The key feature, however, was that the space was divided into two parts. Hidden by a partition, the show was a double runway, a double parade of identical twins walking in parallel formation and wearing copies of the same clothes. Halfway through the show, the central partition rose to the sound of alarm sirens, exposing the other second set of bleachers, the audience and the models walking the runway. For the finale, the twins emerged from opposite sides to meet in the middle and walk along the now joined runway together holding hands, looking 'alike, but not alike'.[37]

The soundtrack added to the theme of twins and doubles. Composed by Gustave Rudman and performed by the Budapest Scoring Orchestra, the music was accentuated by the sound of Marianne Faithful's raspy voice reading the lyrics of 'Identical Twins' (1992) by John Forster. Initially written for Mary Kate and Ashley Olsen, the song speaks to the eeriness of twinhood, of existing as opposite of another:

I am not a xerox
I am not a clone
A duplicate, a copycat
A second scoop ... on the ice cream cone
[...]
We look a lot alike
But we are not alike
Two...two, totally...totally, utterly...utterly
Opposite...opposite, totally...totally, different...different
Identical twins![38]

While the soundtrack, in its distorted repetition, created a captivating yet uncanny atmosphere, it was the visual duplicate that evoked the show's heightened uncanniness. As Eco writes, 'The peak of the inexplicable and the uncanny is the apparition of our double, the doppelgänger'.[39] The figure of the doppelgänger, or uncanny double, has long occupied a central role in Gothic literature and horror cinema, functioning as a symbol of internal division, repressed desire and existential threat. It disturbs by appearing both familiar and alien, thus embodying Sigmund Freud's concept of the uncanny (*das Unheimliche*) as the return of something once known but repressed. The doppelgänger destabilises the integrity of identity by mirroring the self while simultaneously hinting at its fragmentation. Consequently, Michele's 'Twinsburg' and its staging raises questions about appearance and integrity of identity.

Across the 68 looks, worn by 68 pairs of twins, the collection traversed an expansive stylistic terrain. In a testament to Michele's eclectic and maximalist tendency, the collection combined strict tailoring, chinoiserie embroidery, glamorous sequin-studded eveningwear, retro activewear, and country-style quilting. Garments like the sequined jacket emblazoned with 'FUORI!!!' referenced the Italian gay liberation magazine from the 1970s, *Fronte Unitario Omosessuale Rivoluzionario Italiano*. The stuffed animal handbags shaped like Gremlins, a reference to the mischievous, multiplying creatures from the 1984 cult film, created another reference to the uncanniness of doubles. Their inclusion served not just as playful pop-cultural nostalgia, but as a metaphor for fluid and proliferating identities – core themes in Michele's work.

His preoccupation with gender and the reconfiguration of gendered signifiers was also evident in the design of men's garter pants. Several iterations of trousers were slashed at the thigh to expose the skin, a traditionally feminine aesthetic as it is usually associated with hosiery. This deliberate reconfiguration of masculine attire highlighted Michele's ongoing deconstruction of gender norms, drawing attention to the eroticism and vulnerability of parts of the male body that are usually hidden in menswear. The accessories continued this theme of ambiguity: Faces were adorned with shoulder-length earrings, heavy sunglasses and chain-covered eyewear that highlighted and obscured the face. The accessories were intended to blur the boundaries between self-expression and disguise, between individuality and anonymity – and in its duplicated form, between original and copy. As Michele writes in the show notes:

As if by magic, clothes duplicate. They seem to lose their status of singularity. The effect is alienating and ambiguous. Almost a rift in the idea of identity, and then, the revelation: the same clothes emanate different qualities on seemingly identical bodies. Fashion, after all, lives on serial multiplications that don't hamper the most genuine expression of every possible individuality.[40]

In *Twinsburg*, Michele used the spectacle of fashion to stage a show on sameness and difference, on identity and its uncanny doubling. By pairing each look with a twin, Michele confronted the audience with the dissonance between surface similarity and interior multiplicity, suggesting that identity is always already fragmented and in flux. His exploration of beauty, gender and the body resisted fixed definitions, instead embracing fashion's potential to destabilise and to transform – to enchant the world with each garment, 'celebrating the continuity of all creatures [...] beyond the differences of species, age, gender, class, and identity'.[41] As a farewell to Gucci, *Twinsburg* was not only a culmination of Michele's auteur vision – his eerie and at times uncanny beauty – but a final ode to fashion's ability to unsettle, enchant and affect norms of beauty.

Notes

1 Brian Moeran, 'The Portrayal of Beauty in Women's Fashion Magazines', *Fashion Theory* 14, no. 4 (2010): 492, https://doi.org/10.2 752/175174110X12792058833933.

2 Umberto Eco, ed., *Die Geschichte der Schönheit* (München: Carl Hanser Verlag, 2019), 298.

3 A. S. Kline, 'Selected French Poems of the 19th Century'. *Poetry in Translation*, 2007, https://www.poetryintranslation.com/PITBR/ French/SelectedFrenchPoemsoftheNineteenthCentury.php#anchor_ Toc160272721.

4 Vicki Karaminas and Justine Taylor, 'Harry Styles: Fashion's Gender Changeling', in *Fashionable Masculinities. Queer, Pimp Daddies and Lumbersexuals*, ed. Vicki Karaminas, Adam Geczy, and Pamela Church Gibson (New Brunswick, New Jersey: Rutgers University Press, 2022), 16.

5 Sarah Mower, 'Gucci Resort 2019', *Vogue*, 30 May 2018, https:// www.vogue.com/fashion-shows/resort-2019/gucci.

6 Alexander Fury, 'Death Becomes Her: Gucci, and Fashion's Immortality Immorality', *AnOther*, 2018, https://www.anothermag. com/fashion-beauty/10897/death-becomes-her-gucci-and-fashions-immortality-immorality.

7 Caroline Evans, *Fashion at the Edge: Spectacle, Modernity and Deathliness* (New Haven and London: Yale University Press, 2003), 297.

8 Benjamin quoted in Susan Buck-Morss, *The Dialectics of Seeing: Walter Benjamin and the Arcades Project* (Cambridge, Massachusetts and London, England: The MIT Press, 1989), 101.

9 Gucci. 'Gucci Hallucination'. *Gucci*, 2025b, accessed 14 May 2025, https://www.gucci.com/us/en/st/stories/article/spring-summer-2018-ignasi-monreal?srsltid=AfmBOoppe0OpFJTIEYWyYaUXjJc bWbiNa9FK3XZIFnFAx5TB-5bKfl-A.

10 Sarah Mower, 'Gucci Fall 2018 Read-To-Wear', *Vogue*, February 21 2018, https://www.vogue.com/fashion-shows/fall-2018-ready-to-wear/gucci.

11 Adam Geczy and Vicki Karaminas, 'The Fashion Chamber and the Posthuman Dissolution of Gender', in *Staging Fashion: The Fashion Show and Its Spaces*, ed. Tiziana Ferrero-Regis and Marissa Lindquist (London: Bloomsbury Visual Arts, 2021), 53, 61.

12 Paul Jobling, Philippa Nesbitt, and Angelene Wong, *Fashion, Identity, Image* (London and New York: Bloosmbury Visual Arts, 2022), 116.

13 Ibid., 125.

14 Tiziana Cardini, 'The Meaning—and the Makers—Behind the Fantastical Special Effects at Alessandro Michele's Gucci Show', *Vogue*, 21 February 2018, https://www.vogue.com/article/gucci-fall-2018-makinarium-special-effects.

15 Emanuele Coccia and Alessandro Michele, *Das Leben der Formen: Eine Philosophie der Wiederverzauberung*, trans. Thomas Stauder (München: Hanser, 2025), 214, my translation.

16 Ibid., 214.

17 Jobling, Nesbitt, and Wong, *Fashion, Identity, Image*, 135.

18 Coccia and Michele, *Das Leben der Formen: Eine Philosophie der Wiederverzauberung*, 215.

19 Donna J. Haraway, 'A Cyborg Manifesto', in *Manifestly Haraway* (ProQuest Ebook Central: University of Minnesota Press, 2016), 67.

20 Patrizia Calefato, *The Clothed Body*, trans. Lisa Adams (Oxford: Berg, 2004), 30.

21 Mikhail Bakhtin, *Rabelais and His World*, trans. Helene Iswolsky (Bloomington: Indiana University Press, 1984), 317–318.

22 Coccia and Michele, *Das Leben der Formen: Eine Philosophie der Wiederverzauberung*, 220–221.

23 Hannah Arendt, *The Human Condition*, 2nd ed. (Chicago & London: The University of Chicago Press, 1958), 7.

24 Coccia and Michele, *Das Leben der Formen: Eine Philosophie der Wiederverzauberung*, 220.

25 Sandra Welte, 'Masked Venice Unveiled: The Venetian Art of Identity Construction', *Working Papers in Social and Cultural Anthropology* 25 (2017): 8.

26 Ingrid Loschek, *Reclams Mode- und Kostümlexikon* (Stuttgart: Reclam, 2011), 282.

27 Coccia and Michele, *Das Leben der Formen: Eine Philosophie der Wiederverzauberung*, 54–55.

28 Ibid., 160.

29 Ibid., 162–163.

30 Hannah Arendt, 'Introduction – Walter Benjamin: 1892–1940', in *Walter Benjamin: Illuminations*, ed. Hannah Arendt (New York: Schocken Books, 1968), 50–51.

31 Ibid., 51.

32 Walter Benjamin, *The Arcades Project*, trans. Howard Eiland and Kevin McLaughlin (Cambridge, Massachuestts, and London, England: Belknap Press of Harvard University Press, 2002), 462.

33 Coccia and Michele, *Das Leben der Formen: Eine Philosophie der Wiederverzauberung*, 163–164.

34 Tiziana Cardini, 'Gucci Resort 2023', *Vogue*, 16 May 2022, https://www.vogue.com/fashion-shows/resort-2023/gucci.

35 Tiziana Ferrero-Regis and Marissa Lindquist, 'Introduction', in *Staging Fashion: The Fashion Show and Its Spaces*, ed. Tiziana Ferrero-Regis and Marissa Lindquist (London: Bloomsbury Visual Arts, 2021), 1–2.

36 Coccia and Michele, *Das Leben der Formen: Eine Philosophie der Wiederverzauberung*, 249.

37 Nicole Phelps, 'Gucci Spring 2023 Ready-to-Wear', *Vogue*, 23 September 2022, https://www.vogue.com/fashion-shows/spring-2023-ready-to-wear/gucci.

38 Forster, John, Mary Kate and Ashley Olsen. 'Identical Twins'. Genius, 1992. https://genius.com/Mary-kate-and-ashley-olsen-identical-twins-lyrics.

39 Umberto Eco, ed., *On Ugliness* (New York: Rizzoli, 2007), 322.

40 Coccia and Michele, *Das Leben der Formen: Eine Philosophie der Wiederverzauberung*, 250.

41 Ibid., 184.

Chapter 3

HACKING HERITAGE

Much has been written on the role of the fashion designer, their artistic abilities and the myth of the creative genius. Ever since its entry into the academy and its sociological and philosophical examination, fashion has been a topic of debate. While it has often been dismissed and criticized for its supposedly ephemeral and frivolous character, the idea of the fashion designer themselves as a creative genius on par with the role of the artist pervades the twentieth century. There are many structural parallels between the art and fashion industries, in particular, the alignment of early twentieth-century couturiers with the figure of the artist, such as Charles Frederick Worth and Paul Poiret. By transforming luxury dressmaking into a professional and masculinized practice, these couturiers elevated garments to the status of art objects, reinforcing their exclusivity and cultural prestige.[1] This art-like status of couture, however, obscures the collaborative nature of fashion design. In truth, fashion is a collaborative creative practice. Recent designers and scholars have challenged this myth, framing the designer instead as a creative director within a broader network of artistic fields and production.[2] This re-framing aligns with critiques of auteur theory in cinema, which similarly overlooks filmmaking's collective labour. Still, just as auteur theory identifies directors with a distinctive visual language, fashion auteurs can also be recognized for their cohesive and identifiable aesthetic, shaped through and sustained by collaboration.

Alessandro Michele bridges the gap between the creation of a recognizable aesthetic and collaboration in his designs – even though Michele himself refrains from calling his approach collaboration. In an interview, he clarifies that collaboration for him is just a semantic convention. Instead, he describes his collaborative work as relevant to his design approach, always putting together and layering 'disparate "talking elements"':

> Introducing multiple, often discordant references has always been inherent to my narration. Metaphorically speaking, it is as if I had drawn a moustache on Mona Lisa's face. My language is eclectic, and it needs many words, many images coming from other people and from other worlds. [...] As far as I'm concerned, from time to time I feel the need to play with someone else.[3]

Michele's concept of collaboration mirrors what Vanessa Gerrie has identified as the borderless fashion practice that characterizes the metamodern and contemporary fashion designer. Borderless fashion designers expand their fashion practice by collaborating with creative practitioners from various fields such as architecture, choreography, graphic design, art or science.[4] Or, in Michele's words, it is a *modus operandi* 'that represents the contemporary world so well; to be open to different languages is a sign of our times'. Consequently, (high) fashion, which has often been defined by exclusivity 'has opened up, welcoming forays coming from other places and other spaces'.[5]

It is no surprise that one of Michele's earliest and most recognizable collaborations comes from a place that Gucci, with its previous jet set image, would have tried to avoid: street art and graffiti. For the Fall/Winter 2016/2017 collection, Michele invited New-York-City-based artist Trevor Andrew, also known as GucciGhost to collaborate and co-design garments for the runway show. Andrew, who began his career as a professional snowboarder, competing in the 1998 and 2002 Winter Olympics, turned to music and art after an injury. As the story goes, his alter ego GucciGhost originated as a last-minute Halloween costume in 2012, dressed in a Gucci blanket with cut-outs for the eyes. He began to spray paint his GucciGhost logo around New York City until Michele met him through the photographer Ari Marcopoulos and asked to him to collaborate. The result was a playful mix of leather accessories, handbags, shoes and ready-to-wear clothes with a graffiti version of the iconic double G monogram pattern in light blue with added yellow stars.

The double G monogram was introduced in the early 1970s and was a variation of the house's original rhombus pattern that adorned its suitcases in the 1930s. Other accessories were sprayed with a diamante, referencing the replacement of its original name Rombi or rhombus with the Italian name *diamante* during Frida Giannini's tenure at the brand; or slogans like 'real' Gucci, or 'egg' (spelled with the inverted double G).

Other memorable collaborations between Michele and other artists include the Fall/Winter 2017/2018 capsule collection with British artist Helen Downie, also known as Unskilled Worker, whose floral patterns and illustrations adorned bags, accessories and dresses, or the collaboration with Spanish illustrator Ignasi Monreal for the 'Gucci Hallucination' campaign for Spring/Summer 2018. The collection, itself inspired by a visit to Elton John's archive of 1970s glam rock looks, was an amalgamation of glitter costumes, shoulder pads, English tweed and track suits, chiffon dresses and tailored suits. In Monreal's illustration, these designs found their way into a reimagination of classic artworks such as John Everett Millais' *Ophelia* (1852), Hieronymus Bosch's *The Garden of Earthly Delights* (1490–1500) or *The Arnolfini Portrait* (1434) by Jan van Eyck. Despite the different design languages between GucciGhost's ironic and street art aesthetic, Unskilled Worker's floral and playful illustrations, or Ignasi Monreal recontextualizing approach, they all seem to fit Michele's 'new' Gucci aesthetic and eclecticism perfectly.

No list of Michele's collaborations would be complete without Harry Styles who became an ambassador for the brand. The British singer-songwriter and former member of British boy band One Direction and the Italian designer share a deep friendship and collaborative relationship. The pair met shortly after Michele had become creative director of Gucci and the musician started his solo career. For all of the promotional material and music videos for Styles' eponymous first solo album released in 2017, he wore Gucci. During the accompanying tour, Styles reinforced his images as a fashion and gender changeling,[6] wearing a variety of gender-fluid, floral and glittery suits of which many were custom designs by Michele. For the Gucci Fall/Winter 2018 tailoring campaign shot by Glen Luchford, a dandified Styles was photographed alongside children and farm animals, wearing embellished suits and dressing gowns and fostering a gender-fluid aesthetic. In 2019, then, Michele and Styles became co-chairs for the Met Gala ball, 'Camp: Notes on Fashion', with Styles wearing high-waisted pants and sheer black organza blouse with ruffled sleeves, and Michele wearing metallic pink pants and a blouse with several rows of frills on the front.

Their friendship and collaborative efforts culminated in the 2022 capsule collection Gucci HA HA HA. The collection merged traditional English tailoring with romantic details like mother-of-pearl buttons and bohemian 1970s influences. Its title, a combination of their initials, was intended as a symbol for their shared humour and artistic dialogue. The garments were a mixture of vintage-inspired denim jackets, print pyjamas, bowling shirts, pleated kilts and tailored suits, all expressing a fluid, flamboyant masculinity. Echoing the aesthetic of the dandy, the looks offered a reinterpretation of classic menswear pieces, heralding a 'vision of beauty [...] where complex and nuanced codes are liberated' and recontextualized.[7]

While it has become quite commonplace for fashion designers to collaborate with other artists, musicians or (streetwear) brands, the way their aesthetics seem to fit seamlessly into Michele's design language is also due to his penchant for discordant references and sartorial signifiers, as well as Michele's ironic play on the house's trademark patterns and logos. Already in his first collections for Gucci, Fall/Winter 2015/2016 menswear and womenswear, Michele showed an initially shocking but playful twist on one of Gucci's most iconic design: the horse bit loafer. Founded in 1921 by Guccio Gucci and his wife, Aida Calvelli, the brand began as a leather goods store known for its fine luggage and handbags. Guccio Gucci, who had worked at the Savoy Hotel in London as a liftboy, wanted to combine the artisanal skills of Florentine workshops with the fine elegance of the English jet set. In the 1950s, Gucci started to expand internationally, opening its first American boutique in 1953 on 58th street in Manhattan, New York City. In the same year, Gucci introduced its first loafer design inspired by Native American moccasins. Its signature miniature horse bit detail was a nod to Gucci's connection to equestrianism and a recognizable symbol for their wealthy international clientele. In the following years, the loafers became one of the brand's most successful design, earning them a spot in the permanent collection of New York's Metropolitan Museum of Art.

With his first collection, Michele proved that he does not shy away from transforming and reimagining Gucci's designs or infusing them with other 'talking elements'. In the Fall/Winter 2015/2016 collection, the loafer – originally designed with a U-shaped silhouette of the toe, visible stitching and a closed heel – first appeared in its classic form: the front was made from soft black leather, decorated with the signature golden horse bit detail and visible stitching. The back, however, was left open, like a slipper, and long kangaroo fur was spilling onto the floor (Figure 3.1). The design, which would become a street style favourite amongst celebrities and fashion-conscious people, initially caused a stir. On the one hand, Gucci was criticized for using real fur despite Kering's efforts to position the use of wild kangaroo fur as in line with the company's sustainable fur guidelines. On the other hand, its design was, at first, not received enthusiastically. 'In the beginning, the guys around my office would say, "You adore things that are ugly or strange"', Michele said. 'Like the shoe with the fur. They were saying, "Oh my god, Alessandro is crazy! And you're putting it on a man and a woman! Oh, no!"' Nonetheless, the fur-lined version (there was also a version without fur), became highly sought after and a best seller. As Michele puts it, 'we only sold the crazy ones. People like to be crazy and special and chic!' Or in other words, Michele's unconventional hybrid twist on Gucci's classic loafer was one of the key items that introduced his eclectic,

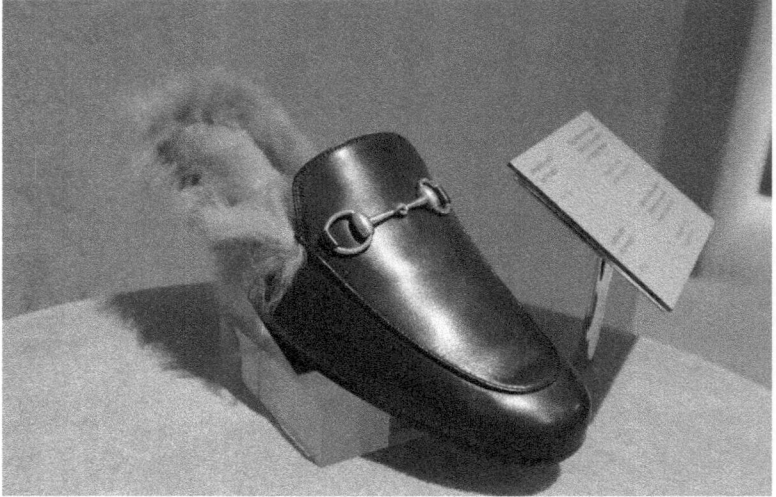

Figure 3.1. Alessandro Michele's re-designed horse bit loafer for Gucci Fall/Winter 2015/2016 with an open back and fur detailing. Gucci Museum, Florence, Italy. 29 December 2023. (Photo: Andrei Antipov/ Shutterstock.com).

magpie aesthetic that encapsulates his idea of beauty, of doing 'the wrong things in the right way'.[8]

Gucci 'Aria', Fall/Winter 2021/2022

Michele's penchant to twist and transform Gucci's signature trademarks and designs reached its peak with the 'Aria' collection, the Fall/Winter 2021/2022 ready-to-wear presented as part of Gucci's centenary celebration. With the world and the fashion industry still marked by the COVID-19 pandemic, the collection was published as a 15-minute film in which the models walked down a runway lined with flashing retro cameras and mingled in a darkened anteroom before stepping outside into an imaginary forest filled with white horses, peacocks and cockatoos. The film was accompanied by a soundtrack that, as Nicole Phelps writes, 'indicates just how deeply the Italian brand has penetrated the zeitgeist'.[9] So much so, that popular music has become a vehicle to spread the Gucci word from Lil Pump's rap song 'Gucci Gang' (2017) that features the rapper attending Gucci High School with his gang dressed head to toe in Gucci to South African rap duo Die Antwoord's hit single 'Gucci Coochie' (2016), featuring American burlesque dancer and model Dita Von Teese. In 2021, a total of 22.705 songs featured the Italian brand since its launch in 1921.[10] Some of these lyrics also found their way onto handbags and sweaters, such as 'Music is Mine Gucci Seats Reclined' from Eric B. & Rakim 'The R' (1988) or 'This One's Dedicated To All You Gucci Bag Carriers Out There It's Called You Got Good Taste' from 'You Got Good Taste' by The Cramps (1983). This was not the first time for Michele to reference Gucci's pop-cultural influence: For the Gucci Cruise 2018 collection, Michele wore a T-shirt with the slogan 'Guccify Yourself' in reference to 'Gucci' becoming a popular slang term meaning 'cool' or 'good' and 'Guccify' meaning 'to bling out; to add high-end qualities to a product or service (or outfit); to make something overly impressive, expensive, or elaborate'.[11] However, in a somewhat surprising twist for Gucci's anniversary collection, Michele 'guccified' not only the house's own symbols and history, but incorporated Demna Gvasalia's Balenciaga characteristics into his idiosyncratic design.

The Gucci brand emphasized this was not a collaboration between the two Kering-owned houses but the result of Michele's so-called 'hacking lab made of incursions and metamorphoses'.[12] The result was a remake of Balenciaga's most well-known shapes and signs of recent years, juxtaposed with Gucci symbolism: the padded hip jacket and skirt combination from Gvasalia's debut Fall/Winter 2016/2017 collection became a crystal-studded silver set with 'Balenciaga' and 'Gucci' lettering all over. Another version was made from one of Gucci's most iconic prints, the 'Flora'. The print, originally designed by artist and set designer Vittorio Accornero for a scarf gifted to actress and Princess Grace of Monaco in 1966, was later chosen as one of the leitmotifs for Gucci's first prêt-a-porter collection in 1981. For the centennial collection, Michele placed the print all over Balenciaga's recognizable sharp tailoring and 'Hourglass' bag. The Balenciaga voluminous puffer jacket from the Fall/Winter 2016/2017 collection – styled on the runway as if it would fall off the shoulders – was reimagined as an off-shoulder utility jacket with the Gucci double G print and contrasting Balenciaga logo. Balenciaga's Spring/Summer 2017 purple spandex peplum top and leggings were 'hacked' with Gucci's signature green and red stripe and GG monogram pattern.

Besides the mixing and 'hacking' of Balenciaga's symbolism, Michele also looked at Gucci's design history and codes. One of the recurring themes was the house's equestrian connection that appeared as horse-riding gear, including riding boots, helmets embellished with the words 'Savoy Club' in reference to Guccio Gucci's liftboy days and bridles and whips carried as equestrian accessories. Some models cracked their whip while walking down the runway. Like the cracking of whips, other equestrian codes were turned into objects of desire, giving them a fetishist twist: harnesses and leather collars were worn over dresses and shirts. Some were decorated with Gucci's horse bit, sprawled across the chest or tightened around the shoulders, others were turned into headgear resembling bridles. One of Tom Ford's most iconic designs for Gucci, the red velvet tuxedo from the Fall/Winter 1996/1997 collection famously worn on the red carpet by Gwyneth Paltrow, was also 'hacked' and reimagined as versions for men and women with pronounced shoulders and styled with a leather harness (Figure 3.2).

This was not the first time that Michele's design teetered on the brink of fetish wear and sadomasochism and bondage (BDSM) symbolism. The Fall/Winter 2019/2020 and the Fall/Winter 2020/2021 collections also included different versions of the harnesses, collars and leather masks. The latter paired with 1980s-inspired power suits, grandfather-style knitted vests, see-through dresses, ruffled XL-skirts, and Peter Pan collars. Like the Fall/Winter 2020/2021 menswear collection,

Figure 3.2. Tom Ford's velvet suit design for Gucci Fall/Winter 1996/1997 was reimagined by Alessandro Michele for the 'Aria' collection, Gucci Fall/Winter 2021/2022, with a leather harness. Gucci Museum, Florence, Italy. 29 December 2023. (Photo: Andrei Antipov/ Shutterstock.com).

the ready-to-wear collection played with sartorial codes from childhood, including school uniforms and preadolescent attire. Here, staging and fetish accessories gave the show a ritualistic and ceremonial character. Titled 'The Ritual', the collection was presented on a large circular platform where the 60 models were dressed and made up by stylists that are usually hidden behind the stage, a 'collective intelligence [that] was strenuously engaged in the ritual of dressing'.[13] For Michele, this ritual is sacred, a magical moment that extends ordinary reality – a sacredness he compared to the ritual of going to the cinema: The beginning and end of the show was accompanied by a voiceover from Italian film director and screenwriter Federico Fellini talking about the communal experience of watching a film at the cinema:

a hypnotic suggestion, something ritualistic, religious. You left the house, parked your car somewhere after a short drive, and then joined a kind of ritual procession: After purchasing your ticket, the curtain opened onto the dimly lit auditorium, where you recognized a few friends. Then the light dimmed, the screen illuminated, and the revelation began.[14]

With the unveiling or rather display of the ritual of dressing the models for a fashion show, as well as the comparison to the cinema, Michele not only elevated the hidden acts of dressing and make-up touches but spoke to the pleasures of seeing – and being seen. As he commented in a post-show interview, the audience was also 'our show, and we were your show'.[15] In his musings on the collection, Michele speaks to the struggles and hidden processes behind the creative act, 'the womb', as he writes, 'the place where poetry takes shape'. Therefore, he wanted to dismantle the wall between audience and creators and 'reverse the perspective to make the invisible visible'.[16]

The use of BDSM and fetish wear accessories fits well with the ritualistic and ceremonial character of the show, revealing to us something that is usually hidden. In the realm of BDSM relationships, rituals, protocols and ceremonies, such as the collaring ceremony, hold significant symbolic meaning and often revolve around clothing and acts of dressing and undressing. Overall, Michele's use of harnesses and leather accessories linked to BDSM symbolism gives his collections an eerie and sometimes slightly out-of-place character. In the case of the 'Aria' collection and the hacking of Gucci's equestrian symbolism, the house's heritage pieces and signs are lifted from its high-society, jet set context and placed into Michele's fantasy world. In the designer's words, 'The myth of foundation is reinhabited in the light of the present'.[17]

This present, for Michele is a playground of cultural, historical and sexual signs that co-exist and talk to each other, while also speaking to the erotic drama of fetishism and fashion that Valerie Steele asserts in her book *Fetish: Fashion, Sex, and Power*

(1996). As Steele writes, the meaning of the clothes designed by fashion designers reproducing the look of fetishism depends on the context and the players, 'fantasy, or imagination, is inevitably about the forbidden and the impossible'. In other words, fetishism in fashion ultimately speaks to 'our ambivalences about what seems to be a disappearing boundary between the "dominate values" and the "perverse"'.[18]

For Michele and his fantasy world, however, it seems to be less about finding a balance between signs of dominant values and the perverse, and more about the coexistence and simultaneousness of all kinds of signs, of Gucci's heritage symbols (GG monogram pattern, horse bit), real-life places (The Savoy Hotel), horse riding gear and fetish wear alongside Balenciaga symbolism, sharp tailoring, retro silhouettes and flowing skirts and dresses. In Michele's 'hacking' universe, the forbidden and impossible are not just a fantasy but reality: Michele's men and women are jet set celebrities, equestrians, office worker, club dancer, nature enthusiasts and lovers. Like the musicians in the songs featured on the soundtrack to the video for the Fall/Winter 2021/2022, Michele is well versed in sampling soundbites and talking elements (or fashion signs and symbols), not just making these his own, but offering a fantasy world and dreamscape where various characters and narratives exist and where everyone can participate: 'It's a playground that we can share all together'.[19]

Gucci x Adidas, Fall/Winter 2022/2023

In 2022, after an already successful collaborative capsule collection with US-outdoor brand The North Face, Gucci introduced another collaboration with a world-famous sports brand: Adidas (Figure 3.3). For the Fall/Winter 2022/2023 collection, Michele hijacked the German sportswear brand's trademark stripes and trefoil icon, merging traditional tailoring and sportswear codes. Several tailored suits were equipped with Adidas' three stripes, as well as baseball caps and beret hats. A cape, a green coat and a crochet set including a balaclava

Figure 3.3. A bag and jacket from Gucci's collaboration with German sportswear brand Adidas. Milan, Italy. 25 June 2022. (Photo: photo-lime/Shutterstock.com).

also featured the brand's iconic trademark symbol. There were several cut-up Adidas sweats turned into corsets, and an ivory satin gown with a ruffled hem and neck and puffy bishop sleeves, evoking the DIY and upcycling aesthetic popular in online forums and social media during the pandemic.

In reference to a dress worn by Madonna in 1993, which Michele mentioned as a source of inspiration, there was a similar red V-neck dress with Adidas stripes along the sides. The original dress, designed by Laura Whitcomb, was one of the first collaborations with the sportswear brand. Label NYC, Whitcomb's streetwear brand that emerged within the 1990s DIY movement, aimed to blur the lines between high and low culture, establishing an inclusive space that critically examined the influence of branding and its pervasive grip on society. Accordingly, Label 'sought to recontextualize the icons and phenomenologies of consumer culture, retooling their energy to tell new stories [that seek] to dismantle a blinding psychic hold'.[20] In Michele's collection, the icons and phenomenologies of consumer culture are recontextualized once more in merging and mixing Gucci's luxury fashion brand with Adidas' sportswear codes.

Titled 'Exquisite Gucci', the collection referenced the Surrealist parlour game *Cadavre Exquis*, a collaborative method in which disparate images or phrases are assembled to form a composite whole – often revealing unexpected connections. By invoking this technique, Michele once more emphasizes his creative process rooted in fragmentation, collaboration, and the subversion of linear coherence. In the show notes, Michele mentions the mirror as a reference for the collection, particularly the distorting magic mirrors of the Baroque cabinets of curiosities. These mirrors create bizarre optical illusions: eyes vanish from faces, trees multiply into forests, human forms morph into horses and gods acquire multiple heads. Consequently, the runway was lined with distorting mirrors, fracturing and transforming the models walking along the catwalk. It is this 'celebration of metamorphosis, in which the playful mechanics of light refraction transcend every spatial boundary' that marks Michele's fascination with mirrors, which is also inhabited by clothes. As Michele writes, a garment is

> a magic mirror par excellence, capable of re-enchanting our presence in the world. For clothing possesses the ability to reflect our image in an expanded and transfigured dimension. [...] garments offer themselves as operators of multiplicity. Wearing them means crossing a transformative threshold where we become something else.[21]

This something else, in Michele's world then, can be an evening gown with sportwear codes, tailored suits with Adidas stripes, or a disparate combination of blue leather boots with lace stockings and body worn with a fur coat, large sunglasses and beret hat. While Michele's references, codes and signifiers come from different worlds, aesthetics and times, in Michele's fashion design, these codes are reassembled into a compelling whole.

Notes

1 Nancy J. Troy, *Couture Culture: A Study in Modern Art and Fashion* (Cambridge, MA: The MIT Press, 2002).

2 Vanessa Gerrie, *Borderless Fashion Practice: Contemporary Fashion in the Metamodern Age* (New Jersey: Rutgers University Press, 2023); Lou Stoppard, *Fashion Together: Fashion's Most Extraordinary Duos on the Art of Collaboration* (New York: Rizzoli, 2018).

3 Tiziana Cardini, 'Alessandro Michele Talks Adidas x Gucci and Other Dream Collaborations—"From Time to Time I Feel the Need to Play With Someone Else"', *Vogue*, 7 June 2022, https://www.vogue.com/article/alessandro-michele-talks-adidas-gucci-and-his-dream-collaborator.

4 Gerrie, *Borderless Fashion Practice: Contemporary Fashion in the Metamodern Age*, 46.

5 Cardini, 'Alessandro Michele Talks Adidas x Gucci and Other Dream Collaborations'.

6 Vicki Karaminas, and Justine Taylor, 'Harry Styles: Fashion's Gender Changeling', in *Fashionable Masculinities. Queer, Pimp Daddies and Lumbersexuals*, ed. by Vicki Karaminas, Adam Geczy and Pamela Church Gibson (New Brunswick, New Jersey: Rutgers University Press, 2022), pp. 9–25.

7 Gucci. 'Gucci Ha Ha Ha'. *Gucci*, 2025a, accessed 2 June 2025, https://www.gucci.com/us/en/st/stories/article/gucci-ha-ha-ha.

8 Lynn Hirschberg, 'Alessandro Michele Reflects on Making a Gucci Collection in One Week', *W Magazine*, 2 February 2020, https://www.wmagazine.com/story/gucci-alessandro-michele-interview.

9 Nicole Phelps, 'Gucci Fall 2021 Ready-to-Wear', *Vogue*, 15 April 2021, https://www.vogue.com/fashion-shows/fall-2021-ready-to-wear/gucci.

10 Gucci. 'Gucci 100'. *Gucci*, 2022a, accessed 17 March 2025, https://www.gucci.com/at/de/st/stories/article/gucci-100-shoppable?srsltid=AfmBOorFwDRvAmW1T2K2JTJDTfErI3VRmIXZ46vIACJaCRZ9l6vNUb5l.

11 'guccify', Urban Dictionary, 2025, accessed 17 March, 2025, https:// www.urbandictionary.com/define.php?term=guccify.

12 Gucci. 'Lingering over the Edge of the Beginning'. *Gucci*, 2022c, accessed 17 March 2025, https://www.gucci.com/at/en_gb/st/ stories/article/aria-fashion-show-details?srsltid=AfmBOoq2ijA5fisB 7gMDyM0Q-w7CuRwZdyuvRQIwG4IrMxJdWHklN9bJ.

13 Emanuele Coccia, and Alessandro Michele, *Das Leben Der Formen: Eine Philosophie Der Wiederverzauberung.* trans. Thomas Stauder (München: Hanser, 2025), 164–165, my translation.

14 Ibid., 229.

15 Nicole Phelps, 'Gucci Fall 2020 Ready-to-Wear', *Vogue*, 19 February 2020, https://www.vogue.com/fashion-shows/fall-2020-ready-to-wear/ gucci.

16 Coccia and Michele, *Das Leben der Formen: Eine Philosophie der Wiederverzauberung*, 164.

17 Gucci, 'Lingering over the Edge of the Beginning'.

18 Valerie Steele, *Fetish: Fashion, Sex, and Power* (Oxford: Oxford University Press, 1996), 55, 197.

19 Phelps, 'Gucci Fall 2021 Ready-to-Wear'.

20 Whitcomb, Laura. 'Gucci's Hommage to Label's Adidas Collaboration Circa 1993'. Designer Laura Whitcomb of Label NYC, n.d. Accessed 12 May 2025, https://www.labelbylaurawhitcomb.com.

21 Coccia and Michele, *Das Leben der Formen: Eine Philosophie der Wiederverzauberung*, 243.

Chapter 4

MAISON VALENTINO

By the end of 2022 and not long after Alessandro Michele took on Gucci's centennial collection, the designer left the Italian fashion house. During a two-year break from the fashion stage, Michele dedicated his time to renovating the 800-year-old Palazzo Scapucci in Rome – a project that fits all too well with the designer's fluid and nonlinear conception of time and places. 'I'm not convinced time passes as the calendar or the clock describes it', he said, 'The 800 years of these walls are *right now* to me'.[1]

Michele's fascination for the past and old, forgotten things, are not only part of his design aesthetic, but were a key component in his revolution at Gucci that was 'a guileless disposition toward untold stories, incursions into the past live of ancient artifacts, monuments, and people'.[2] It is not surprising, then, that Michele took the same approach of looking into the past to Valentino. The designer showed his first collection, Valentino Resort 2025, just two months after his appointment as creative director for the Roman fashion house. Initially, the collection was supposed to be released into stores, but in a surprise Zoom call with selected fashion editors, Michele published a lookbook in June 2024 for the 171 ready-to-wear designs, including an additional 93 images of shoes, bags and various accessories.

As Michele recounts, he felt seduced by the Maison and the 'marvellous quantity of objects in the archive'.[3] Even though Valentino's archive does not reach back 100 years as does Gucci, the brand's history includes a vast range of collections and labels including an Haute Couture label. In November 1959, after he had trained in Paris at the *Ecole de la Chambre Syndicale de la Couture*, Valentino Garavani opened his first studio in Rome. After the Second World War, the Italian city had become the centre for the Italian Alta Moda and, as film studios like Cinecittà produced many blockbuster movies, Valentino began to dress Hollywood's elite stars including Rita Hayworth, Elizabeth Taylor, Audrey Hepburn and Sophia Loren.

In 1960, Valentino and his then-partner Giancarlo Giammetti founded the Maison Valentino. In the summer of 1962, Valentino showed at the Pitti Salon in Florence, where the fashion world had moved by then, before finally settling in Milan. In 1968, Valentino made a name for himself with his *Collezione Bianca*, a series of white gowns and coats bearing the distinctive V that would become his trademark. That same year, Jacqueline Kennedy ordered her wedding dress for her wedding to Aristotle Onassis from Valentino. Giammetti proved to be a skilled business manager; with his support, Valentino launched his ready-to-wear line in 1970 and simultaneously introduced an accessories line. Five years later, he showed his ready-to-wear in Paris and established the Maison there permanently.

Besides the infamous *Bianca* collection, Valentino introduced a lush, poppy red in his collections that would become known as Rosso Valentino, or Valentino red. Having visited the opera in Barcelona, he became infatuated with the vibrant colour. 'All the costumes on the stage were red', he said later. 'All the women in the boxes were mostly dressed in red, and they leant forward like geraniums on balconies, and the seats and drapes were red too […]. I realised that after black and white, there was no finer colour'.[4]

In 2007, at the age of 75, Valentino retired from the fashion world. After his retirement, Alessandra Facchinetti took over, before Maria Grazia Chiuri and Pierpaolo Piccioli assumed creative direction of the house and since 2016, Piccolio has been solely responsible for the creative direction. Like Valentino, Piccolio promoted a singular colour at the Maison, the so-called Valentino Pink, a magenta shade almost like a fluorescent neon. The Fall/Winter 2022/2023 collection was entirely designed in this Valentino pink. His tenure ended in March 2024 when Michele took over.

Valentino Resort 2025

For his first collection for Valentino, Michele once again hacked the brand's archive and reintroduced and reassembled Valentino designs into his own maximalist, vintage aesthetic. Particularly Garavani's designs from the 1960s, 1970s and 1980s which were a starting point for Michele, who is frequently drawn to that era of fashion history. Consequently, the resort collection included an array of 1970s duster and trench coats with fur-lined cuffs and hems. Several skirts and blouses featured ruffles and pleats, hound-tooth checks and geometric prints embellished capes and jackets, and long, sequined gowns evoked the glamourous evening gowns Valentino designed for Hollywood actresses. Knitwear and denim pieces were offset with preppy shorts and polo shirts and, as it is Michele's forte, there was not much distinction between menswear and womenswear.

A few looks also referenced the brand's signature red colour – a belted coat with a high-standing collar, a shrunken sweater with tiny white bows and a chiffon midi dress with a ruffled collar and hem. Other looks featured scattered flower and wallpaper prints, paisley patterns and embroidered flowers. Accessories were abundant and featured rows of pearls, big tear-drop earrings with crystals, and various editions of a draped turban.

The clearest – and for Michele perhaps the simplest reference – came in the form of white and cream-coloured designs inspired by Valentino's *Collezione Bianca* collection. A-line coats and dresses, 1960s box-shaped jackets and miniskirts, straight cut tailored suits and blazers as well as kimono-like jackets and pants combinations appeared in various shades of white, cream and off-white, with many featuring the brand's signature V-detail. Michele also reimagined these pieces with a romantic and eclectic aesthetic with leopard prints and ruffled pussy bow details, re-creating that hippy chic and refinement of 1970s Valentino. 'I stole something of that whiteness, of that grace', he said, 'indulging in the lightness of ruching and volants "for no other reason than to connect with that feeling of grace"'.[5]

Despite this being one of Michele's most streamlined and perhaps cohesive collection – his talking elements and temporal signifiers were mostly limited to Valentino's own archival looks and the 1970s romantic hippie style with cross-cultural references in the form of turbans and a jacket featuring a *pankou* or frog closure – some critics seemed disappointed with Michele's debut at Valentino and its alleged resemblance to his work at Gucci. As Emma Davidson writes 'Michele is arguably the biggest auteur working in fashion right now, [...] But I'll admit I'm shocked by how closely this first collection resembles what he was doing at Gucci'.[6] As I would argue and have done so throughout this book, it is Michele's ability to transfer and translate various sartorial and cultural signifiers into his own eclectic, vintage aesthetic that marks his auteurism. As a fashion auteur, Michele spoke to, and with Valentino's own ideas of beauty, femininity and elegance, merging them into an aesthetically cohesive collection. In contrast to his work at

Gucci, Michele's first Valentino collection was more refined, simplistic and sophisticated as well as an amalgamation of various clothing styles.

Valentino Spring/Summer 2025

The following collection, Valentino Spring/Summer 2025 entitled 'Pavillon des Folies', was a more visible return to Michele's quirky abundance, albeit still more Valentino than Gucci. For the show, the location had moved from the Hôtel Salomon de Rothschild in the 8th arrondissement, where Valentino had shown for several years, to an arena on the Périphérique of Paris. The otherwise plain arena had been decorated with an array of love seats, chairs, ottomans, floor lamps, armoires and birdcages, all hidden under white dust sheets. The floor, covered in cracked mirrors, reflected the ghostly furniture an icy cracked lake that the models' walked over. 'The only thing I really care about is historical places', said Michele, 'I like the places where people died, people lived'.[7] Once more Michele's fashion show was staged in a somewhat liminal temporal space, a space caught between the past and the present, a space that is neither here nor there, used but not used, a space of transition.

The staging, a mixture of abandoned state home and elaborate theatre, also evokes a particular scene from Sally Potter's 1992 *Orlando* starring Tilda Swinton as the gender-bending (and sex-changing) Orlando. Shortly after Orlando changes her sex, stating famously that they are the 'same person, no difference at all, just a different sex', Orlando returns to their stately house in England. Dressed in a voluminous white gown, Orlando walks through one of the parlours, narrowly avoiding the furniture that is covered in white dust sheets. Like this scene in the film, the fashion show plays with the ghostly presence created by the dust covers. As a visual reminder, the covers hint at a previous life, or rather a place once inhabited by people, a past preserved and cocooned to be revealed later, in the present.

It is a very fitting stage for Michele's collection for Valentino that itself seems to have lived through several decades and gone through a metamorphosis to appear in the present. However, in contrast to many of his previous collections, Michele was less inspired by the Renaissance, but more by Valentino's archive and the 1970s and 1980s. The collection was adorned with rows of bows, tassels, feather boas and fur shawls. Valentino pleats and ruffles erupted from collars, decorated hems of dresses or were layered in tiers on skirts and blouses. Some looks, for instance, the strapless purple dress with cascading rows of volants and tiny polka dots and worn with white lace tights, or the floor-length cerulean-blue gown made from silk-chiffon, pleated and ruched and adorned with ruffles along the dropped waist and cascading ruffles around the knees, seemed to be reminiscent of 1980s ball or prom dresses. 'This is him, *with* me. It's *almost* him. I tried to make it a little bit different', Michele explained his way of interpreting and utilizing Valentino's techniques and penchant for pleats. 'Sometimes I try to replicate the same, because it's so fascinating. But I think that we are both in the same dress'.[8]

Similarly, other designs referenced or used the house's archive directly, such as the nut-brown-patterned silk-cloqué fabric used for a calf-length skirt and high-neck blouse worn with a fur-trimmed jacket. While the outfit itself seems to be mostly Valentino, it is in the abundant and unconventional accessories that Michele's design language emerges. The model wore a pair of John Lennon sunglasses with dangling gold sequins along the round frame, a large chunky gold chain necklace with a crystal pendant, 'like a rapper's trophy combined with the prized heirloom of a dowager duchess'.[9] Another outfit consisted of high-waisted, tailored grey pants and a boxy cream-coloured jacket with polka-dot details, a Valentino red satin bow fastening was accessorized with an XL-brimmed straw hat and delicate black see-through gloves. The rather conservative outfit was also worn with a large rhinestone nose ring and a crescent-shaped piercing framing the model's lower lip – another example of Michele's inclusion of a punk aesthetic in contrast to chic vintage looks.

Valentino Haute Couture Spring 2025

In many respects, the Spring/Summer 2025 collection was a precursor for Michele's very first Haute Couture collection that was to follow in January 2025. Entitled 'Vertigineux' (French for dizzying), the collection was a display of Michele's maximalist and eclectic design, mixing and combining references spanning from the Renaissance to the contemporary, from punk and subcultural styles to the carnivalesque and the camp. Presented in the Palais Brongniart, the collection spanned 48 looks worn by models of all kinds of ages and styled with simple make-up and hair. A choice, that, once again, reflects Michele's fluid and boundary-less approach: 'I think it doesn't make sense to put boundaries in the idea of ages', he said to regarding his model casting. 'I like people, so I don't want to make boundaries between human beings'.[10]

In contrast to his previous runways that were turned into surgical operating rooms (Gucci Fall/Winter 2018/2019), offering a glance behind the scenes (Gucci Fall/Winter 2020/2021) or taking place on the Walk of Fame in Los Angeles (Gucci Spring/Summer 2022), the runway for his first couture collection was turned into a black naked stage. Accompanied by choral songs and cold electronic sounds, the runway created was an eerie, liminal space, void of human presence and a space of transition. Lists of inspirations and references ran across the background in digital red letters while at the same time, each look was announced in big, illuminated numbers.

These lists were, as Michele explained in his show notes, the point of departure and kept him company during the making of the collection. Once again citing Italian semiotician Umberto Eco, Michele writes that

> every list shifts between two opposite and complementary tendencies. On one side, it's an attempt to confine the

infinite extension of the existing within a meaningful
framework. [...] On the other side, the list can transcend
into poetry becoming a visionary, aesthetic and narrative
instrument.[11]

Michele refers to Eco's musings on *The Infinity of Lists* (2009).
Accordingly, 'the list is at the origin of culture', an attempt
to 'make the infinite comprehensible', to grasp what is
ungraspable.[12] Practical lists, like inventories, shopping lists or
lists of dinner guests are somewhat finite, an enclosed unit that
carries a primarily practical function defined by the things in
the real world it is referring to. Other lists, such as catalogues
and museum collections, are more poetic. They attempt to
create order, to cope with infinity, but are themselves infinite,
an open-ended list.

For Michele, it is the latter that holds specific meaning
regarding the creation of the 'Vertigineux' collection. In other
words, it was the 'vertigo of the list', the unfinished nature of
catalogues, of lists containing infinite things that pushed him to
imagine every look 'as an uninterrupted and potentially infinite
catalogue of words: an ungrammatical list that proceeds through
accumulation and juxtaposition'.[13] The lists accompanying each
look were projected in an infinite loop, containing both material
and immaterial associations ranging from proportions, fabrics,
colours and botanical and animal references to time periods,
emotions, concepts and literary and historical figures. 'A poetics
of the etcetera', as Michele writes, 'where every thread, every

seam, every trace of colour transfigures into a multiplicity of words that transcend the boundaries of the visible'.[14]

This feeling of vertigo triggered by the infinity of lists was also conveyed in the design of the collection that was an amalgamation of disparate things and references, a plurality of associations and colliding worlds. Starting with the first look, a floor-length evening dress that incorporated a diamond shape in four colours, creating a harlequin pattern made of layered and interwoven tulle in light blue, peachy pink, burgundy red and pea green. The cone-shaped skirt, held in shape by a large crinoline, was also rushed with layered tulle (Figure 4.1). Although this clownish, carnivalesque design might not be the first association one might have with Valentino, the original reference was once again the Maison's archive. A reimagining of Valentino's Spring/Summer 1992 couture collection showed a similar dress in a slimmer silhouette and different colours. Thus, the look was accompanied by a list of words including dramaturgy, diamonds, medieval mysteries and Valentino Garavani.

This reimagining of archival looks, emphasizing, enlarging and making it his own, while juxtaposing other elements and references is what Michele does best. Consequently, other looks were also taken from Valentino's archive, reimagined in Michele's contemporary aesthetic. A black, narrow strap dress with a light blue panel at the hips from the Spring 1985 collection was reworked with an exaggerated Rococo-style crinoline flaring out at the waist and flowing downwards; a red

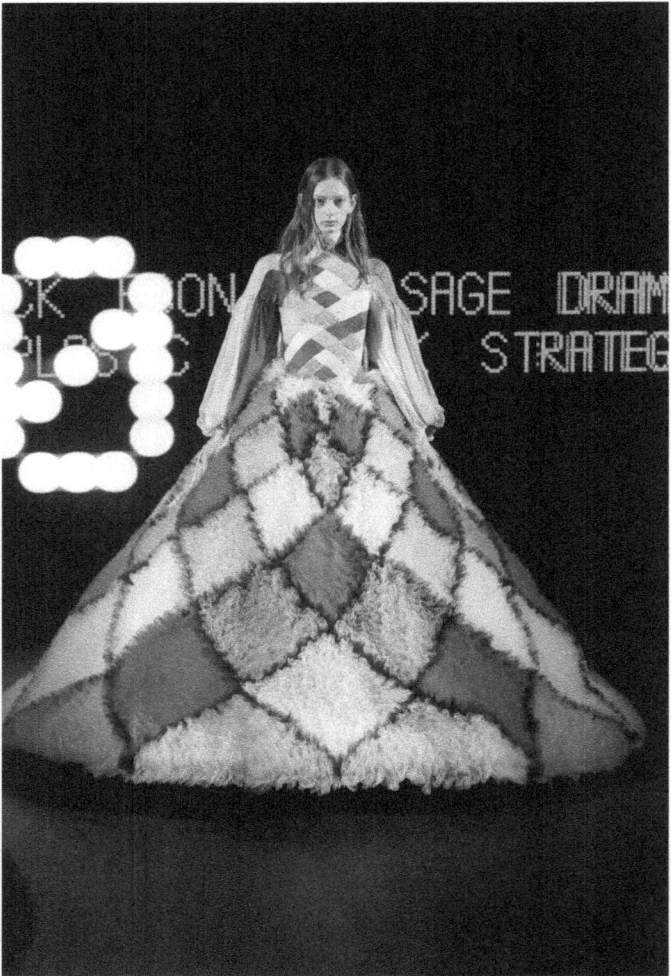

Figure 4.1. Look 1 from the Valentino Spring/Summer Haute Couture 2025 show. The model is wearing a tulle dress with a crinoline and diamond-shaped pattern. (Photo: Shutterstock).

evening dress from the Fall/Winter 1977 couture collection, was reimagined with a padded and embroidered boxy vest reminiscent of Spanish bullfighter jacket, the *Chaquetilla*, with rushed sleeves, XL tulle ruffles and a dropped waist; a pink Robe Manteau with piping along the front from the 1970s was reworked into a rich green eighteenth-century dress including a pannier underneath and ruffled sleeve hems.

Sarah Mower said that Michele's debut couture collection felt 'like being involved in a cinematic psychodrama – swept along in one man's stream of fevered imaginings'.[15] These imaginings involved a variety of humorous and exaggerated proportions and accessories resembling the 'carnivalesque techniques of inversion, travesty and upset proportions which were central to carnival humour'.[16] As Mikhail Bakhtin writes,

This is why in carnivalesque images there is so much turnabout, so many opposite faces and intentionally upset proportions. We see this first of all in the participants' apparel. Men are transvested as women and vice versa, costumes are turned inside out, and outer garments replace underwear. The description of charivari of the early fourteenth century, in Roman du Fauvel, says of its participants, 'They donned all their garments backwards'.[17]

As Bakhtin also notes, inversion plays a key role in many forms of comic expression, which can be seen as acts of cultural resistance or rejection. As cultural anthropologist Barbara Babcock explains, '"symbolic inversion" may be broadly defined as an act of expressive behaviour which inverts, contradicts, abrogates, or in some fashion presents an alternative to commonly held cultural codes, values, and norms', which could be 'linguistic, literary, or artistic, religious, or social and political'.[18] In other words, through the rejection of established systems and orders, and the deliberate disruption of categorical and classificatory frameworks, inversions may be interpreted as enacting a critique of closed symbolic systems and the rigidity of fixed categories. The latter is what drives Michele's aesthetic inversions, not least with the disruption of the gender binary or temporalities as discussed in Chapter 1 of this book, but also with his carnivalesque couture collection, that has, like the carnivalesque imagery, 'so much turnabout, so many opposite faces and intentionally upset proportions'.

Besides his reimagining of Valentino's archival looks and techniques – including tiny pleats on trumpet sleeves, delicate, intricate ruffles and floral prints, bows, ruffled blouse slits and jewelled latticework – Michele exploded the shapes and proportions by layering enormous crinolines, hoop skirts and panniers underneath. Clownish imagery of the Harlequin was also abundant: clownish cone hats, harlequin patchwork patterns and ruff collars adorned almost every other look and were juxtaposed with delicate and intricate pleating or embroidery.

Speaking on his design approach – a floor length gown with tapestry embroidery, a large crinoline and an embroidered mask covering the models head and face – Michele explains: 'I'm trying to make it like a sculpture [...] [it] could be 1950 tapestry. It could be the dress of Elizabeth I, and [it] could be a joke. [It] could be a kid that makes a dress with mom's carpet in the dining room'.[19] The mask, in particular, was a recurring theme in his debut couture collection, echoing Michele's musings on the freedom of masquerades and changing of identity in the Venetian Carnival. Masks appeared as delicately embroidered lace, as embroidered and jewelled wrestling masks or as elaborate head pieces covering the face in rows of rhinestones.

One of the most symbolically inverted looks might be look 37, a high-necked moiré robe with a wide pleated skirt and white lace hem and train. The robe was inspired by the red dress worn by clergy and priests around Rome, as Michele explained: 'When I was a kid, it was the most beautiful dress I saw walking in the street – really beyond – on a man. You see priests in a restaurant, the market. They eat, laugh, even smoke'.[20] The priest's robe in Michele's collection was reimagined as a constructed evening gown worn with rhinestones cascading down from glittering frames to extend past the chin and white laced glove, creating a playful, parodic yet eerie symbolic inversion on a religious and cultural code. Fittingly, the list accompanying this look included words like heresy, profanation, Rome, transcendence, iconography, altar boy.

Michele's 'Vertigineux' collection resembles or mirrors what Bakhtin theorized as part of the laughter celebrated by the carnival of the Renaissance, 'the spectacular feast of inversion and parody of high culture' which he sees as 'the possibility of a "complete withdrawal from the present order"'. Or, as Renate Lachmann writes,

> in the carnivalesque game of inverting official values he sees the anticipation of another, utopian world in which anti-hierarchism, relativity of values, questioning of authority, openness, joyous anarchy, and the ridiculing of all dogmas hold sway, a world in which syncretism and a myriad of differing perspectives are permitted.[21]

For Michele, the carnivalesque image is thus not just the laughter, parody or exaggeration in his designs, but the infinity of lists made visible, unfolding into layers of references and inversions: 'It's a list that unfolds into a burst of combinations, recalls, echoes to the very edge of the speakable. It's the journey into the vertigo of an unfinished multiplicity'.[22] It is a utopian imagination against the or rather as the withdrawal from present order. As Michele states, in our contemporary world with its political and cultural changes and negotiations, 'we need to fight, showing more and more incredible expression of creativity and imagination'.[23]

Valentino Fall/Winter 2025/2026

Michele's symbolic inversion and hacking of the brand's heritage continued in the Valentino Fall/Winter 2025/2026 collection. Staged in a public restroom installation with cubicles and washbasins lining the runway, the room was bathed in red lights and everything from the floor to the ceiling was painted Valentino red. The models, entering through the cubicle doors, sometimes lingered at the basins, looking in the mirrors before vanishing through the cubicles from which they came (Figure 4.2) – a meta-theatre, as Michele puts it, that plays with the expectations of public and private, intimacy and the performance of identity and a true self.

In the show notes, Michele explained his approach to the collection and choice of the public toilet as the stage. Quoting Italian philosopher Romano Màdera, Michele states that the word intimacy and the promise of a true, hidden self are misleading. Rather, 'also the deepest intimacy of all is a theatre [...] a metatheatre in the theatre of existence', which, in itself is a continuous performance. Though Michele does not refer to Erving Goffmann's dramaturgical model of performance, his metaphor of the theatre, the backstage and performance certainly hint at Goffmann's theory of self-presentation and the dramaturgical metaphor of the theatre. What becomes clear in Michele's musings in the show notes, however, is his choice of the public restroom as the stage for the Fall/Winter 2025/2026 collection. Accordingly, he writes:

> I imagined a public toilet: a counter-place that neutralizes and suspends the dualism between inside and outside, between what is intimate and what is exposed, between the personal and the collective, between what remains

Figure 4.2. Runway look from the Valentino Fall/Winter 2025/2026 show. The model, wearing a blue lace dress with pink ruffles around the hip, walks backstage through a cubicle door. (Photo: Shutterstock).

private and what is meant to be shared, between depth and surface. A spatial heterotopia (M. Foucault) where the ritual of caring for intimacies clearly reveals its meta-theatrical dimension.[24]

Here, Michele refers to Michel Foucault's concept of heterotopia to describe spaces and places that exist in our real world, but are also cultural, institutional and discursive spaces that represent, disturb or transform societal norms. As real places (in contrast to utopias that are unreal spaces), heterotopias are 'something like counter-sites, a kind of effectively enacted utopia in which real sites [...] are simultaneously represented, contested, and inverted'.[25] The public restroom is a heterotopia of ritual and purification, a space that is isolated and penetrable but not as freely accessible as public spaces.

However, it was not just the show's installation that questioned the intimacy of a public space, a space of duality and contradiction. The recording also begins with the sound of a toilet flushing and someone knocking on a door, an uncommon start to a fashion show, but an all-too well-known moment of intimacy at any visit to a public restroom. The clothes also questioned and made visible Michele's musings on intimacy, turning the inside out. Thus, the first look showed a carnivalesque inversion of a red lace body worn open at the crotch and under a satin bra. Other looks barely covered the model's breasts with transparent Chantilly lace while necklines of evening gowns were carved out low to show skin.

This (almost) nakedness was contrasted with high-neck shirts and pussy bow blouses, sharp tailoring and all-black outfits that covered the models from head to toe.

The collection, entitled 'Le Méta-Théâtre Des Intimités', was another approach to reinvent and revamp the Valentino brand with Michele's idiosyncratic aesthetic. The result was a mix of Michele's maximalism and disparate cultural references (lace bodies, stacked necklaces and accessories, neckties and ruffs, a cat's face on a crystal-embellished long evening gown) and Valentino's refined yet opulent elegance (sharply tailored suits and coats, built-out shoulders reminiscent of 1980s Valentino, pleated tulle and embellished evening gowns). A sheer, red blouse with lace details seemed to reference Michele's own design from his debut menswear collection at Gucci, while other looks continued the harlequin pattern and print in a more pastel colour scheme.

The result, as Michele writes in the show notes, 'is a dystopian, disturbing, Lynchian space: a temporarily autonomous space, free from the codification of norms, proudly political because it has the potential to subvert any rigid binary classification'.[26] In many ways, Michele here describes his own aesthetic and design language as a fashion auteur. In Michele's intellectual, maximalist and eclectic world, in this 'dystopian, disturbing, Lynchian space', the forbidden and impossible can exist and coexist within the dystopia and utopia of possibilities: Gucci's heritage symbols, riding gear and Valentino's opulent elegance exist alongside fetish codes, pop-cultural references and the carnival. From model's partying in an imagined Savoy club, frolicking in the forest together with horses and peacocks, to eerie liminal spaces, haunted by the ghostly presence and absence of the past and the present – Michele's auteur world is a space of temporal and cultural subversion, of coexistence of possibilities and absence of classifications, a true Michelean space.

Notes

1 Chiara Barzini, 'Inside Alessandro Michele's Otherworldly Apartment in Rome', *Vogue*, 28 November 2023, https://www.vogue.com/article/alessandro-michele-apartment-rome.

2 Ibid.

3 Luisa Zargani, 'Alessandro Michele Surprises, Unveiling First Designs for Valentino in Resort Collection', *Women's Wear Daily*, 17 June, 2024, https://wwd.com/runway/resort-2025/milan/valentino/review/.

4 Brenda Polan and Roger Tredre, *The Great Fashion Designers: From Chanel to McQueen, the Names that Made Fashion History*, 2nd ed. (London: Bloomsbury Visual Arts, 2020), 176.

5 Tiziana Cardini, 'Valentino Resort 2025', *Vogue*, 17 June 2024, https://www.vogue.com/fashion-shows/resort-2025/valentino#review.

6 Maliha Shoaib and Lucy Maguire, 'The industry verdict on Alessandro Michele's Valentino debut', *Vogue Business*, 18 June 2024, https://www.voguebusiness.com/story/fashion/the-industry-verdict-on-alessandro-micheles-valentino-debut.

7 Rebecca Mead, 'When In Rome: Inside Alessandro Michele's New Vision For Valentino', *Vogue*, 29 January 2025, https://www.vogue.co.uk/article/alessandro-michele-valentino-interview.

8 Ibid.

9 Ibid.

10 Vogue, 'Inside Valentino's Haute Couture Atelier With Alessandro
   Michele | Vogue', (9:27: YouTube, 2025), Video, 8:00 mins. https://
   www.youtube.com/watch?v=fcOtX3mCjeg.

11 maisonvalentino (maisonvalentino), 'The list and its poetic potential',
   Instagram, 29 January 2025, slide 2, https://www.instagram.com/
   maisonvalentino/p/DFaS2RpsjV2/?img_index=2.

12 Ibid, slide 1.

13 Ibid., slide 3.

14 Ibid.

15 Sarah Mower, 'Valentino Spring 2025 Couture', *Vogue*, 29 January
   2025, https://www.vogue.com/fashion-shows/spring-2025-couture/
   valentino.

16 Francesca Granata, 'Mikhail Bakhtin: Fashioning the Grotesque
   Body', in *Thinking Through Fashion: A Guide to Key Theorists*, ed. Agnès
   Rocamora and Anneke Smelik (London: I.B.Tauris, 2016), 107.

17 Mikhail Bakhtin, *Rabelais and His World*, trans. Helene Iswolsky
   (Bloomington: Indiana University Press, 1984), 410–11.

18 Barbara A. Babcock, *The Reversible World: Symbolic Inversion in Art and
   Society* (Ithaca, NY: Cornell University Press, 1978), 14.

19 Vogue, 'Inside Valentino's Haute Couture Atelier With Alessandro
   Michele | Vogue', 6:41.

20 Mower, 'Valentino Spring 2025 Couture'.

21 Renate Lachmann, 'Bakhtin and Carnival: Culture as Counter-Culture',
   Cultural Critique, no. 11 (1988): 118, https://doi.org/10.2307/1354246,
   http://www.jstor.org/stable/1354246.

22 maisonvalentino, 'The list and its poetic potential', slide 3.

23 Vogue, 'Inside Valentino's Haute Couture Atelier With Alessandro
   Michele | Vogue', 8:48.

24 maisonvalentino (maisonvalentino), "'No intimacy can ultimately undress us, no veil can be torn to put us before our true self'", *Instagram*, 9 March 2025, slide 1, https://www.instagram.com/maisonvalentino/p/DG-7k4Eotwz/?img_index=1.

25 Michel Foucault, 'Of Other Spaces', *Diacritics* 16, no. 1 (1986): 24, https://doi.org/10.2307/464648, http://www.jstor.org/stable/464648.

26 maisonvalentino, "'No intimacy can ultimately undress us, no veil can be torn to put us before our true self'", slide 1.

Conclusion

ON HOLLYWOOD

In November 2021, when the fashion industry returned to in-person presentations after several seasons of virtual experiences due to COVID-19 restrictions, Michele showed Gucci's Spring/Summer 2022 collection not in Milan, where they staged most of the shows, but in Los Angeles, on the Hollywood Boulevard. Hollywood's *Walk of Fame*, the infamous walkway celebrating stars from film, television and the entertainment industries, turned into the stage for Gucci's 'Love Parade' – a collection that, as Nicole Phelps writes, has 'never made more sense than this one [...] on Hollywood Boulevard, with its neon lights and Walk of Stars'.[1]

Michele's fascination for Hollywood, cinema and visceral storytelling culminated in this collection that featured, beside its mix of old Hollywood glamour, sharp tailoring and clashing prints and patterns, several of Gucci's unconventional celebrity friends, including Macaulay Culkin, Miranda July, Jodie

Turner-Smith and Jared Leto. Leto, a long-time collaborator of Michele, previously appeared alongside the designer on the Met Gala carpet, dressed as his twin or carrying a replica of his own head. The clothes fit perfectly into Michele's fashion auteur world, embodying his signature tension between spectacle and subversion, nostalgia and provocation – a vivid blend of traditional tailoring and athleisure, Hollywood glamour and Californian ease, streetwear and cowboy aesthetics. Key looks featured wide-lapelled tailored jackets paired with brightly coloured ribbed-knit and see-through lace leggings and sneakers. Others played with erotic codes: Skintight latex garments appeared alongside sheer lace dresses and chiffon gowns; hand-held accessories, necklaces and jewellery resembling sex toys suggested a tongue-in-cheek commentary on desire, fashion and fetishism, evoking once again a subtle BDSM aesthetic. In other words, Gucci's Spring/Summer 2022 collection offered a polymorphous mix of sartorial signs and contrasting aesthetics – a cinematic fantasy.

As we have seen throughout this book, Michele's fascination for cinema and Hollywood is threaded through his work, from use of cinematic and special effects in the Cyborg collection, to his frequent references to the all-encompassing storytelling and ritual of the cinema. Influenced by his mother's work at a production company in Rome, Hollywood, for Michele, is more than a place of cinematic production. It is, as he writes, 'essentially a Greek temple inhabited by pagan gods. Here, actors and actresses are celebrated like mythological heroes:

hybrid creatures who combine divine transcendence and mortal existence, imagination and reality'.[2] Consequently, Hollywood and the cinema have influenced Michele's own understanding of fashion and his approach to its design. For Michele, 'cinema is life as absolute fashion: its seemingly impossible version, the disguise that opens a crack in the waking state and fills it with dreams under the open sky'.[3]

Alessandro Michele's tenure at Gucci represents one of the most significant creative shifts in twenty-first-century fashion. Through a radical reimagining of sartorial language, he not only redefined the aesthetic identity of a heritage luxury house, but reshaped the cultural meanings embedded in dress. This book has explored Michele's work through the lens of the fashion auteur: a fashion designer whose philosophy and visual storytelling extend beyond garments to encompass a total world-building practice. What emerges from Michele's work is a distinct narrative voice, one defined by its devotion to ambiguity, multiplicity and transformation.

Chapter 1 explored Michele's gender and temporal fluidity, starting from his debut at Gucci in 2015, Michele broke from the hyper-sexualized aesthetic of his predecessor and signalled a new queer, intellectual and vintage-inflected sensibility. The red pussy bow blouse and floral suiting, worn by both male and female models, became emblems of a new gender-fluid language that would define his work. Michele's early collections were discussed as acts of sartorial *détournement* – a recontextualization of disparate signs. Drawing from thinkers such as Giorgio Agamben and Walter Benjamin, this book argued that Michele's nonlinear conception of time – where past, present and future coexist in contemporary relation – subverts normative narratives of progress and newness in fashion. Michele's aesthetics of abundance and maximalism, positioned against minimalist norms in luxury fashion, foregrounds the complexity, contradiction and excess of identity construction. His use of archival prints, vintage silhouettes and references to historical periods transforms fashion into sites of reassembled history, where old meanings are pulled from obscurity, recontextualized and given new meaning in a nonlinear now.

Chapter 2 explored Michele's conception of beauty, theatricality and the use of fashion shows as immersive, dramaturgical spaces. Here, the runway becomes a performative stage in which fashion is presented not only as a commercial product but as a site of mythmaking and spectacle. Drawing on the shows from Fall/Winter 2018/2019, Fall/Winter 2020/2021, and Spring/Summer 2023 – ranging from posthuman laboratories to uncanny doppelgänger parades – this chapter argued that Michele uses the fashion show to question and destabilize conceptions of beauty and identity categories, particularly those around gender, the body, and the self. These collections foreground the mask, the double and the cyborg, emphasizing fashion's entanglement with performance, prosthesis, and the uncanny. In Michele's fashion design and staging, identity is not only performative, but complex, contradictory and always in flux.

The final two chapters explored Michele's work as a fashion auteur in collaboration with other brands, their archives and other artists and designers. From hacking Balenciaga's and Adidas' aesthetic codes, to expanding on and proliferating Valentino's archive, the chapters discussed how Michele operates as a fashion auteur: curating and constructing a visual identity with foreign languages and sartorial signs, creating a narrative fashion firmly situated within his Michelean world. A world that combines and simultaneously celebrates erotic codes, heritage symbolism, carnivalesque imagery and inversion.

Taken together, these chapters illuminate the multidimensionality of Michele's design and the expansive cultural significance of his work. His fashion design resists clear categorization: it is at once archival and futuristic, flamboyant and intellectual, romantic and unsettling. Through a language of visual citation, symbolic layering, and aesthetic maximalism, Michele's collections do not merely reflect the zeitgeist, they challenge and recontextualize it. His fashion design does not offer a final answer on gender, time, or identity; rather, it visualizes these categories as unstable, fluid and always in the process of becoming. In doing so, he creates room for a multiplicity of subjects to emerge – of subjectivities that do not conform to the linear narratives of fashion or history, but who exist, like his own fashion design, in constellation – as dreams under the open sky. In Michele's fashion auteurism, these dreams become possibilities filled with ambiguity and multiplicities, creating a world in which everything seems possible.

Notes

1 Nicole Phelps, 'Gucci Spring 2022 Ready-to-Wear', *Vogue*, 2 November 2021, https://www.vogue.com/fashion-shows/spring-2022-ready-to-wear/gucci.

2 Emanuele Coccia and Alessandro Michele, *Das Leben der Formen: Eine Philosophie der Wiederverzauberung*, trans. Thomas Stauder (München: Hanser, 2025), 241.

3 Ibid., 156.

APPENDIX

Timeline

1972   November 25: Alessandro Michele is born in Rome, Italy.

1990s   Studies costume design at the *Accademia di Costume e di Moda* in Rome and graduates in the early 1990s.

1994   Moves to Bologna and begins working at the Italian knitwear company Les Copains.

1997   Joins Fendi in Rome, working in the accessories department under Karl Lagerfeld and Silvia Venturini Fendi.

2002   Recruited by Tom Ford (creative director of Gucci from 1994 to 2004) to join Gucci in London, working in the accessories division. Works alongside Frida Giannini, head of handbags and accessories at the time.

2006   Promoted to senior designer of leather goods at Gucci.

2011   Becomes associate creative director under Frida Giannini, creative director of Gucci since 2005.

2014   Appointed creative director of Richard Ginori, a Florentine porcelain manufacturer founded in 1735 and acquired by Gucci in 2013.

2015   January: Marco Bizzarri, CEO of Gucci, asks Michele to act as interim creative designer for the menswear show. Debuts first menswear collection for Gucci (Fall/Winter 2015/2016) a week later on January 19.

January 21: Announced as new creative director of Gucci. First creative director to be responsible for menswear and womenswear collections, accessories, eyewear, jewellery and children's wear, the beauty and fragrance departments, advertising, digital and social media platforms as well as store design.

February 25: Debuts first womenswear collection as newly appointed creative director (Fall/Winter 2015/2016).

November: Receives the International Designer Award from the British Fashion Council.

2016   April: Gucci announces to join the shows for womenswear and menswear collections.

June: Receives International Award from the Council of Fashion Designers of America (CFDA).

September: Named GQ Designer of the Year at the GQ Men of the Year Awards in London.

2017   April: Michele is listed as one of TIME's 100 most influential people.

July: Launches Gucci Décor, the brand's first homeware line.

September: Designs custom stage outfits for Harry Style's first solo tour, Live on Tour.

2018   January: Reopens the Gucci Museum in Florence, Italy as the Gucci Garden, featuring a boutique, art gallery, cinema and restaurant.

February 21: Debuts the Gucci 'Cyborg' collection (Fall/ Winter 2018/2019), including looks featuring duplicates of models' heads.

October: Co-curated with Maurizio Cattelan the Gucci art exhibition 'The Artist is Present' in Shanghai.

2019   Co-chairs the 2019 Met Gala 'Camp: Notes on Fashion' together with Harry Styles, Lady Gaga, Serena Williams and Anna Wintour.

2020   April 15: Gucci's 'Aria' collection celebrated the house's 100th anniversary. The collection features sartorial codes from Balenciaga.

2022   November: Michele departs Gucci after nearly eight years as creative director.

2024   March 28: Valentino announces the appointment of Michele as creative director. He replaced Pierpaolo Piccioli who exited the brand one week earlier.

2025   January 29: Debuts first Haute Couture collection for Maison Valentino during Paris Haute Couture Week.

REFERENCES

Agamben, Giorgio. 'What Is the Contemporary?'. In *'What Is an Apparatus?' And Other Essays*, edited by Werner Hamacher. Meridian: Crossing Aesthetics Series, 39–56. Stanford: Stanford University Press, 2009.

Arendt, Hannah. *The Human Condition*. 2nd ed. Chicago & London: The University of Chicago Press, 1958.

————. 'Introduction – Walter Benjamin: 1892–1940'. Translated by Harry Zohn. In *Walter Benjamin: Illuminations*, edited by Hannah Arendt, 1–55. New York: Schocken Books, 1968.

Babcock, Barbara A. *The Reversible World: Symbolic Inversion in Art and Society*. Ithaca, NY: Cornell University Press, 1978.

Bakhtin, Mikhail. *Rabelais and His World*. Translated by Helene Iswolsky. Bloomington: Indiana University Press, 1984.

Barzini, Chiara. 'Inside Alessandro Michele's Otherworldly Apartment in Rome'. *Vogue*, 28 November 2023. https://www.vogue.com/article/alessandro-michele-apartment-rome.

Benjamin, Walter. *The Arcades Project*. Translated by Howard Eiland and Kevin McLaughlin. Cambridge, MA and London: Belknap Press of Harvard University Press, 2002.

Beyer, Judith. *Antigender Fashion: The Possibilities of Gender-Fluid and Non-Binary Fashion Design*. London: Bloomsbury Visual Arts, 2025.

―――. 'Beyond the Binary: A Close Reading of Gender-Fluid Masculinities in Gucci's Spring/Summer 2016 Campaign'. *Journal of Bodies, Sexualities, and Masculinities* 4, no. 1 (2023): 125–48. https://doi.org/10.3167/jbsm.2023.040108.

―――. 'Out of Reach: Gucci's 'Tian' Suit between Material Culture and Gender-Fluid Imagination'. *Clothing Cultures* 11, no. 1 (2024): 65–83. https://doi.org/10.1386/cc_00079_1.

Blanga-Gubbay, Daniel. 'The Distance with the Present. On Agamben's Notion of the Contemporary'. *Documenta* 34, no. 2 (2020): 90–100. https://doi.org/10.21825/doc.v34i2.16387.

Blanks, Tim. 'Gucci Fall 2015 Menswear'. *Vogue*, 19 January 2015. https://www.vogue.com/fashion-shows/fall-2015-menswear/gucci.

―――. 'Gucci Spring 2016 Menswear'. *Vogue*, 22 June 2015. https://www.vogue.com/fashion-shows/spring-2016-menswear/gucci.

Bowles, Hamish. 'Inside the Wild World of Gucci's Alessandro Michele'. *Vogue*, 15 April 2019. https://www.vogue.com/article/gucci-alessandro-michele-interview-may-2019-issue.

Britten, Fleur. 'Take a Bow: Kate Moss Outfit Sends Subversive Message at Depp Libel Trial'. *The Guardian*, 27 May 2022. https://www.theguardian.com/film/2022/may/27/kate-moss-outfit-johnny-depp-amber-heard-trial.

Buck-Morss, Susan. *The Dialectics of Seeing: Walter Benjamin and the Arcades Project*. Cambridge, MA and London: The MIT Press, 1989.

Butler, Judith. *Gender Trouble: Feminism and the Subversion of Identity*. New York: Routledge, 2006. First published 1990.

————. *Who's Afraid of Gender?* Great Britain: Allen Lane/Penguin Books, 2024.

Calefato, Patrizia. *The Clothed Body.* Translated by Lisa Adams. Oxford: Berg, 2004.

Cardini, Tiziana. 'The Meaning – and the Makers – Behind the Fantastical Special Effects at Alessandro Michele's Gucci Show'. *Vogue*, 21 February 2018. https://www.vogue.com/article/gucci-fall-2018-makinarium-special-effects.

————. 'Gucci Resort 2023'. *Vogue*, 16 May 2022. https://www.vogue.com/fashion-shows/resort-2023/gucci.

————. 'Alessandro Michele Talks Adidas X Gucci and Other Dream Collaborations – "from Time to Time I Feel the Need to Play with Someone Else"'. *Vogue*, 7 June 2022. https://www.vogue.com/article/alessandro-michele-talks-adidas-gucci-and-his-dream-collaborator.

————. 'Valentino Resort 2025'. *Vogue*, 17 June 2024. https://www.vogue.com/fashion-shows/resort-2025/valentino#review.

Cheang, Sarah, Erica de Greef, and Yoko Takagi. *Rethinking Fashion Globalization.* London: Bloomsbury Visual Arts, 2021.

Church Gibson, Pamela. 'The Rough and the Smooth Revisited: Masculinity, Fashion, and James Bond for a New Millennium'. In *Fashionable Masculinities. Queer, Pimp Daddies and Lumbersexuals*, edited by Vicki Karaminas, Adam Geczy and Pamela Church Gibson, 137–149. New Brunswick, NJ: Rutgers University Press, 2022.

Coccia, Emanuele, and Alessandro Michele. *Das Leben Der Formen: Eine Philosophie Der Wiederverzauberung.* Translated by Thomas Stauder. München: Hanser, 2025.

Craik, Jennifer. 'Exotic Narratives in Fashion: The Impact of Motifs of Exotica on Fashion Design and Fashionable Identities'. In *Modern Fashion Traditions: Negotiating Tradition and Modernity through Fashion*, edited by M. Angela Jansen and Jennifer Craik, 97–118. London: Bloomsbury Academic, 2018.

Debord, Guy. 'Definitions'. Edited and Translated by Ken Knabb. In *Situationist International Anthology*, 51–52. Berkeley, CA: Bureau of Public Secrets, 2006.

Deleuze, Gilles, and Félix Guattari. *A Thousand Plateaus: Capitalism and Schizophrenia*. London and New York: Continuum, 2004.

Ebert, Michael, and Sven Michaelsen. 'Alessandro Michele: Das Interview'. *Fashion Icons*, Die Gucci Story – Wie Alessandro Michele die Modewelt verändert, no. 01 (2019): 14–27.

Eco, Umberto, ed. *Die Geschichte Der Schönheit*. München: Carl Hanser Verlag, 2019.

———, ed. *On Ugliness*. New York: Rizzoli, 2007.

Evans, Caroline. *Fashion at the Edge: Spectacle, Modernity and Deathliness*. New Haven and London: Yale University Press, 2003.

Ferrero-Regis, Tiziana, and Marissa Lindquist. 'Introduction'. In *Staging Fashion: The Fashion Show and Its Spaces*, edited by Tiziana Ferrero-Regis and Marissa Lindquist, 1–13. London: Bloomsbury Visual Arts, 2021.

Forster, John, Mary Kate and Ashley Olsen. 'Identical Twins'. *Genius*, 1992. https://genius.com/Mary-kate-and-ashley-olsen-identical-twins-lyrics.

Foucault, Michel. 'Of Other Spaces'. *Diacritics* 16, no. 1 (1986): 22–27. https://doi.org/10.2307/464648. http://www.jstor.org/stable/464648.

Fury, Alexander. 'Death Becomes Her: Gucci, and Fashion's Immortality Immorality'. *AnOther*, 31 May 2018. https://www.anothermag. com/fashion-beauty/10897/death-becomes-her-gucci-and-fashions-immortality-immorality.

Geczy, Adam. *Fashion and Orientalism: Dress, Textiles and Culture from the 17th to the 21st Century*. London: Bloomsbury Academic, 2013.

Geczy, Adam, and Vicki Karaminas. 'The Fashion Chamber and the Posthuman Dissolution of Gender'. In *Staging Fashion: The Fashion Show and Its Spaces*, edited by Tiziana Ferrero-Regis and Marissa Lindquist, 58–70. London: Bloomsbury Visual Arts, 2021.

———. 'Power + Fashion'. *Foucault Studies*, no. 36 (2024): 201–26. https://doi.org/10.22439/fs.i36.7230.

Gerrie, Vanessa. *Borderless Fashion Practice: Contemporary Fashion in the Metamodern Age*. New Jersey: Rutgers University Press, 2023.

Goldsmith, Sarah. 'Marble Marvels and Classical Ideals'. In *Fashioning Masculinities: The Art of Menswear*, edited by Rosalind McKever, Claire Wilcox and Marta Franceschini, 26–43. London: V&A Publishing, 2022.

Granata, Francesca. 'Mikhail Bakhtin: Fashioning the Grotesque Body'. In *Thinking through Fashion: A Guide to Key Theorists*, edited by Agnès Rocamora and Anneke Smelik, 97–114. London: I.B.Tauris, 2016.

Griggs, Brendon. 'America's Transgender Moment'. *CNN*, 1 June 2015. https://edition.cnn.com/2015/04/23/living/transgender-moment-jenner-feat/index.html.

Gucci. 'Gucci 100'. *Gucci*, 2022a, accessed 17 March 2025, https://www.gucci.com/at/de/st/stories/article/gucci-100-shoppable?srsltid=Af mBOorFwDRvAmW1T2K2JTJDTfErI3VRmIXZ46vIACJaCRZ 9l6vNUb5l.

———. 'The Future Is Fluid'. *Gucci* 2022b, accessed 31 March 2025, https://www.gucci.com/us/en/st/stories/article/chime-for-change-the-future-is-fluid-film?srsltid=AfmBOopVnREZRI9x32_5dCQwi QWQASCQZbVf8PeRjK6jbxjM14f2QgQB.

———. 'Lingering over the Edge of the Beginning'. *Gucci*, 2022c, accessed 17 March 2025, https://www.gucci.com/at/en_gb/st/stories/article/aria-fashion-show-details?srsltid=AfmBOoq2ijA5fisB 7gMDyM0Q-w7CuRwZdyuvRQIwG4IrMxJdWHklN9bJ.

———. 'Gucci Ha Ha Ha'. *Gucci*, 2025a, accessed 2 June 2025, https://www.gucci.com/us/en/st/stories/article/gucci-ha-ha-ha.

———. 'Gucci Hallucination'. *Gucci*, 2025b, accessed 14 May 2025, https://www.gucci.com/us/en/st/stories/article/spring-summer-2018-ignasi-monreal?srsltid=AfmBOoppe0OpFJTIEYWyYaUXjJc bWbiNa9FK3XZIFnFAx5TB-5bKfl-A.

'Guccify'. Urban Dictionary, 2025, accessed 17 March 2025, https://www.urbandictionary.com/define.php?term=guccify.

Halberstam, Jack. *Trans**: A Quick and Quirky Account of Gender Variability*. Oakland: University of California Press, 2018.

Haraway, Donna J. 'A Cyborg Manifesto'. In *Manifestly Haraway*, 5–90. ProQuest Ebook Central: University of Minnesota Press, 2016.

Hirschberg, Lynn. 'Alessandro Michele Reflects on Making a Gucci Collection in One Week'. *W Magazine*, 2 February 2020. https://www.wmagazine.com/story/gucci-alessandro-michele-interview.

Kline, A. S. 'Selected French Poems of the 19th Century'. Poetry in Translation, 2007, https://www.poetryintranslation.com/PITBR/French/SelectedFrenchPoemsoftheNineteenthCentury.php#anchor_ Toc160272721.

Jobling, Paul, Philippa Nesbitt, and Angelene Wong. *Fashion, Identity, Image*. London and New York: Bloomsbury Visual Arts, 2022.

Karaminas, Vicki, and Justine Taylor. 'Harry Styles: Fashion's Gender Changeling'. In *Fashionable Masculinities. Queer, Pimp Daddies and Lumbersexuals*, edited by Vicki Karaminas, Adam Geczy and Pamela Church Gibson, 9–25. New Brunswick, NJ: Rutgers University Press, 2022.

Kering. '2015 Results'. news release, 19 February 2016, https://www.kering.com/en/news/2015-results-solid-full-year-performances/.

———. *2021 Financial Document*. Kering (Kering, 17 February 2022). https://www.kering.com/api/download-file/?path=Kering_2021_Financial_Document_ENG_4fa3b7a30c.pdf. Accessed 2 June 2025.

———. 'Alessandro Michele Stepping down as Gucci's Creative Director'. *Kering*, 2022, accessed 27 January 2025, https://www.kering.com/en/news/alessandro-michele-stepping-down-as-gucci-s-creative-director/.

Kramer, Elizabeth. 'New Vintage – New History? The Sukajan (Souvenir Jacket) and Its Fashionable Reproduction'. *International Journal of Fashion Studies* 7, no. 1 (2020): 25–47. https://doi.org/10.1386/infs_00015_1.

Lachmann, Renate. 'Bakhtin and Carnival: Culture as Counter-Culture'. *Cultural Critique*, no. 11 (1988): 115–52. https://doi.org/10.2307/1354246. http://www.jstor.org/stable/1354246.

Leitch, Luke. 'Gucci Fall 2020 Menswear'. *Vogue*, 14 January 2020. https://www.vogue.com/fashion-shows/fall-2020-menswear/gucci.

Loschek, Ingrid. *Reclams Mode- und Kostümlexikon*. Stuttgart: Reclam, 2011.

maisonvalentino. 'The List and Its Poetic Potential'. *Instagram*, 29 January 2025. https://www.instagram.com/maisonvalentino/p/DFaS2RpsjV2/?img_index=2.

———. '"No Intimacy Can Ultimately Undress Us, No Veil Can Be Torn to Put Us before Our True Self."' *Instagram*, 9 March 2025. https://www.instagram.com/maisonvalentino/p/DG-7k4Eotwz/?img_index=1.

Maoui, Zak. 'Gender Fluid Fashion Is the Future. Here's How Menswear Is Changing'. *GQ*, 27 November 2018. https://www.gq-magazine.co.uk/article/gender-fluid-clothing.

Mauriès, Patrick. *Androgyne: Fashion + Gender*. London: Thames & Hudson, 2017.

Mead, Rebecca. 'When in Rome: Inside Alessandro Michele's New Vision for Valentino'. *Vogue*, 29 January 2025. https://www.vogue.co.uk/article/alessandro-michele-valentino-interview.

Moeran, Brian. 'The Portrayal of Beauty in Women's Fashion Magazines'. *Fashion Theory* 14, no. 4 (2010): 491–510. https://doi.org/10.2752/175174110X12792058833933.

Mower, Sarah. 'Gucci Fall 2017 Ready-to-Wear'. *Vogue*, 22 February 2017. https://www.vogue.com/fashion-shows/fall-2017-ready-to-wear/gucci.

———. 'Gucci Fall 2018 Read-to-Wear'. *Vogue*, 21 February 2018. https://www.vogue.com/fashion-shows/fall-2018-ready-to-wear/gucci.

———. 'Gucci Resort 2019'. *Vogue*, 30 May 2018. https://www.vogue.com/fashion-shows/resort-2019/gucci.

———. 'Valentino Spring 2025 Couture'. *Vogue*, 29 January 2025. https://www.vogue.com/fashion-shows/spring-2025-couture/valentino.

Phelps, Nicole. 'Gucci Fall 2015 Ready-to-Wear'. *Vogue*, 25 February 2015. https://www.vogue.com/fashion-shows/fall-2015-ready-to-wear/gucci.

———. 'Gucci Fall 2020 Ready-to-Wear'. *Vogue*, 19 February 2020. https://www.vogue.com/fashion-shows/fall-2020-ready-to-wear/gucci.

———. 'Gucci Fall 2021 Ready-to-Wear'. *Vogue*, 15 April 2021. https://www.vogue.com/fashion-shows/fall-2021-ready-to-wear/gucci.

———. 'Gucci Spring 2022 Ready-to-Wear'. *Vogue*, 2 November 2021. https://www.vogue.com/fashion-shows/spring-2022-ready-to-wear/gucci.

———. 'Gucci Spring 2023 Ready-to-Wear'. *Vogue*, 23 September 2022. https://www.vogue.com/fashion-shows/spring-2023-ready-to-wear/gucci.

Polan, Brenda, and Roger Tredre. *The Great Fashion Designers: From Chanel to Mcqueen, the Names That Made Fashion History.* 2nd ed. London: Bloomsbury Visual Arts, 2020.

Shoaib, Maliha, and Lucy Maguire. 'The Industry Verdict on Alessandro Michele's Valentino Debut'. *Vogue Business*, 18 June 2024. https://www.voguebusiness.com/story/fashion/the-industry-verdict-on-alessandro-micheles-valentino-debut.

Steele, Valerie. *Fetish: Fashion, Sex, and Power.* Oxford: Oxford University Press, 1996.

Stoppard, Lou. *Fashion Together: Fashion's Most Extraordinary Duos on the Art of Collaboration.* New York: Rizzoli, 2018.

Troy, Nancy J. *Couture Culture: A Study in Modern Art and Fashion.* Cambridge, MA: The MIT Press, 2002.

Vogue. 'Inside Valentino's Haute Couture Atelier with Alessandro Michele | Vogue'. 9:27 *YouTube*, 2025. Video. https://www.youtube.com/watch?v=fcOtX3mCjeg.

Welte, Sandra. 'Masked Venice Unveiled: The Venetian Art of Identity Construction'. *Working Papers in Social and Cultural Anthropology* 25 (2017): 1–31.

Whitcomb, Laura. 'Gucci's Hommage to Label's Adidas Collaboration Circa 1993'. 'Designer Laura Whitcomb of Label Nyc'. n.d., accessed 12 May 2025, https://www.labelbylaurawhitcomb.com.

Wingfield, Jonathan. 'The Happy Couple: Marco Bizzarri & Alessandro Michele'. *System Magazine*, Issue 7, 2016. https://system-magazine.com/issues/issue-7/alessandro-michele-marco-bizzarri.

Zacarias, Gabriel. 'Détournement in Language and the Visual Arts'. In *The Situationist International: A Critical Handbook*, edited by Alastair Hemmens and Gabriel Zacarias, 214–235. London: Pluto Press, 2020.

Zargani, Luisa. 'Alessandro Michele Is Exiting Gucci, Sources Say'. *Women's Wear Daily*, 22 November 2022. https://wwd.com/fashion-news/designer-luxury/sources-say-alessandro-michele-exiting-gucci-1235427822/.

———. 'Alessandro Michele Surprises, Unveiling First Designs for Valentino in Resort Collection'. *Women's Wear Daily*, 17 June 2024. https://wwd.com/runway/resort-2025/milan/valentino/review/.

INDEX

www.ingramcontent.com/pod-product-compliance
Lightning Source LLC
Chambersburg PA
CBHW020002290326
41935CB00007B/270